Barbecuing Atlantic Seafood

by Julie Watson

NIMBUS PUBLISHING LIMITED

© 1988 Julie Watson

Nimbus Publishing Limited
P.O. Box 9301, Station A
Halifax, N.S.   B3K 5N5

Canadian Cataloguing in Publication Data

Watson, Julie, 1943-

Atlantic seafood barbecue

ISBN 0-920852-97-1

1. Cookery (Seafood)   2. Barbecue cookery   I. Title.
TX747.W37 1988   641.6'92   C88-098520-8

Design: Etta Moffatt
Typesetting: McCurdy Printing & Typesetting Limited
Printing and Binding: Seaboard Printing
Cover photograph: John Watson

Printed and Bound in Canada

Dedication
For the Abegweit Gang—our
barbecue buddies, Carol and
Russ, Beth and David, Deb and
Tim, Sandy, Jo and Al, and of
course, Jack and John—who
shared in testing and putting up
with windy visits to the shore.

Special thanks to Carol and Russ
for reserving my spot on the
livingroom floor.

CREDITS

As I finalise the manuscript for this collection of seafood barbecue recipes the blue jays keep disrupting my thoughts. Snow has come to our Island home and, they demand, it is time to get those sunflower seeds outside and fill the feeders. So annoyed are they with my tardiness that they settle on the windowsills, pecking the glass. Then, when they lose their grip, wheel up to buzz as close to me as they can.

This is surprisingly near. Enough so to make me shy away from time to time as my computer sits at the window of my office. The snow and ice have turned a drab landscape into something wonderful to behold on this sun-filled winter day.

Soon I must stop typing and venture out to warm up the barbecue. We still have a dozen recipes to test, but that is not the only reason for the barbecue being fired up this evening. I really do have to thank the publisher for pushing me to get this book completed. We had forgotten the joys of cooking outdoors in the winter—a simple case of getting caught in the rat race and forgetting to take time out for life. For taking us back to the great outdoors, we thank Nimbus Publishing.

Along with my gratitude to Nimbus staff, special thanks go to the following who answered my questions, shared information and provided recipes:

Anita Landry, seafood promotion supervisor, New Brunswick Department of Fisheries

Marilyn O'Neil, Nova Scotia Department of Fisheries, New Bedford Seafood Council, Massachusetts

Linda Grieco, Mesquite Wood Canada Inc., Whitby, Ontario.

Cathy O'Brien, Department of Fisheries and Oceans, St. John's Newfoundland

Barb Harmes, Prince Edward Island Department of Fisheries

Kenelm Coons, New England Fisheries Development Foundation Inc., Boston, Massachusetts

Beef Information Centre, Toronto, Ontario

Kasey Wilson of Vancouver, British Columbia for keeping me up on trends

The editors and writers of such fine magazines as Canadian Living, Food and Wine, Woman's Day, Family Circle, Cooks, and many more, whose features inspire me to explore the world of food and try new and wonderful creations.

Table of
Contents

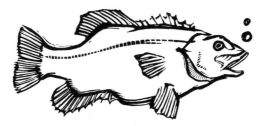

Introduction

B arbecuing is one of the simplest methods of cooking. It is also one of the most satisfying and to my mind the most delicious. There is another plus, at least, to me: it is very social.

Seafood takes naturally to the barbecue for there is none which cannot be cooked over the coals. If there are secrets to success, they are: remember to keep it simple, don't overcook and don't handle or turn the fish any more than is absolutely necessary.

There are a few common-sense rules about barbecuing. Once you know them, and have practised a few times to get to know your own barbecue, it will be a truly relaxing and pleasurable way to cook.

The same applies to seafood; just a few basic methods learned will give you a lifetime of delicious, nutritious eating. Scientists and nutritionists have confirmed what many people around the world have known for centuries, especially the Japanese: fish is good for you. Low in fat, rich in protein, and easily digested, it can be consumed every day of the week. For those concerned about healthy eating, there can be no better cooking appliance than the barbecue and no better food than that from the sea, lakes and rivers.

In this book we are going to learn about cooking over and in the coals. There are many varieties of barbecues, braziers and grills to choose from today. Being a small family who like to pick up and go, we have a portable propane barbecue and a rather battered hibachi.

Recipes in this book have been tested on these two "appliances," and if that isn't proof enough that you don't have to buy the best and most expensive equipment on the market, try these recipes for yourself on your barbecue and decide for yourself whether your equipment is adequate.

I firmly believe you should choose equipment to suit your lifestyle. In our case we live near wonderful beaches and parks. We ourselves enjoy cooking by the shore or, if the weather is inclement, in a sheltered picnic area, and we do this all year round. Also we have many, many visitors each summer who want to do the same thing, so we are portable. I must also tell you that we often cook on the front porch at home.

For people who have attractive yards with decks, patios or pools it is logical to have more permanently located equipment. Think about what you want before you buy yours.

Perhaps the most important thing you have to learn is how to light a fire and judge when it is ready to do the job you want it to do.

About Seafood

FISH—LEAN OR FAT The amount of fat content in fish species is important information for the cook, and also for the consumer. Those with higher fat content often have more flavor, e.g. salmon and mackerel, and, of course, contain more calories. Cod, an example of a lean fish, has less than half the calories of mackerel. Weight loss and nutrition programs laud fish and encourage it as an important portion of one's diet, choosing lean over fat fish.

Scientists are currently studying fish oils to see if in fact by lowering blood cholesterol in humans, fish oils may contribute towards the prevention of heart disease. Certainly high protein, low calories and natural tenderness, and simplicity in preparation make fish a favorite in North America today.

The following list makes three categories of fish, but please note that the medium ones such as shark are in the lean category. This list is not intended as a dietary control, but rather as an aid to choosing marinades.

LEAN

bass
catfish (some)
cod croaker/drum
flounder

pollock (Boston bluefish)
porgy
redfish (ocean perch)
red snapper

grounder
haddock
monkfish
orange roughly
perch (walleye)
pickerel
pike

rockfish scrod
sea bass
shark
shellfish (all)
sole
tilefish
whiting

MEDIUM

hake
halibut
rainbow trout

speckled trout
swordfish
whitefish

FAT

bluefish
butterfish
catfish (some)
eel
herring
mackerel
sablefish

salmon
sardines
shad
squid
striped bass
tuna
turbot

SERVINGS

This general guide will act as an aid in determining **how much fish to buy per serving,** depending of course on appetites.

Whole drawn fish with only the entrail removed 1 lb/454g
Whole dressed fish (head, tail, fins and entrails removed) 8 oz/225g
Steaks (cross-section cuts of larger fish) . . . . 6-8 oz/170-225 g
Fillets (meaty sides of fish cut away from bones) . . . . 5 oz/140 g
Kebabs (chunks for threading on skewers, usually purchased as
steaks or fillets) . . . . 5-6 oz/140-170 g

STORING FRESH FISH

WHOLE FISH
— clean (eviscerate) immediately
— wash in cold water and pat dry with paper towels
— wrap tightly or place in a covered container
— store in refrigerator
— keep no longer than 3 days

FILLETS OR STEAKS
— wipe with a damp cloth
— wrap tightly or place in a covered container
— store in refrigerator
— use as soon as possible, keep no longer than 3 days

If you will not be able to use seafood within 24 hours and cannot plan to purchase fresh for cooking, I suggest you look into freezing. It is simple to do and very successful.

For storing shellfish, see below.

SHELLFISH

Each species of shellfish is different, and needs its own treatment.

SCALLOPS For the purposes of the recipes in this book we have used Sea Scallops, the large variety found in waters off the northern seaboard and in the Gulf of St. Lawrence. Calico Scallops, fished along the eastern coast of Florida are much smaller and are best cooked in a grill basket for a shorter time.

For information on Kamaboko "scallops" see the section "Imitators."

Scallops require approximately 10 minutes cooking time, depending on size. Allow 5 to 8 per person, depending on size. Although very rich in taste scallops have about the same number of calories as haddock for equal size portions. They should be creamy white, moist and have an agreeable, slightly sweetish odor.

CLAMS, MUSSELS If they are going to be eaten straight from the shell, with only a dipping sauce, allow 10-12 per person (more for big eaters); if serving stuffed about half this amount is sufficient.

Fresh clams, mussels and oysters are alive if the shells close tightly when tapped. An open shell should be tapped gently; if it remains open it should be discarded. Cultivated mussels tend to gape more widely, but will also close, although much, much more slowly, when tapped. This method is fine when dealing with small quantities, but can take ages if you have a lot of shellfish. The important thing is to buy from a reliable seafood outlet just before you will be using shellfish. If any of them feel lighter of heavier than average, discard them, and also discard any that don't open fully during cooking.

Clams and mussels in the shell will keep up to 4 days if stored at temperatures 32°-40°F (0°-4°C). If they are packaged in a plastic bag to bring home from the store, open the bag and poke holes in the sides so that they can breath. If they are in a carton (waxed cardboard), refrigerate surrounded by ice.

OYSTERS The oyster has a flat upper shell and a concave or rounded bottom shell which provides a space for the body of the oyster. It is important to recognize this when cooking on the grill as the concave side will hold the juices better than the flat side.

Oysters are frequently eaten raw. An oyster knife is inserted between the shells to pry it apart; once opened, sever the muscle holding the oyster to the shell, remove any particles of shell and the oyster is ready to eat. If you are having trouble getting the knife between the shells, take a hammer and chip off enough of the edge to make the job easier. I suggest wearing a heavy oven mitt or several layers of towel on the hand holding the oyster to prevent scratches and cuts.

The lean rich oyster meat can also be strung on skewers, but don't overcook; they require very little cooking.

If kept at temperatures 32°-40°F (0°-4°C) oysters will remain alive for up to 3 months. Shucked oysters may be kept no longer than 1 to 2 days in the refrigerator at the same temperature.

SHRIMP Fresh shrimp should have a mild pleasant odor and the meat should be firm in texture. The shell covering should fit closely to the body; if the body has shrunk from the shell, the shrimp may not be fresh. Good signs are mild odor, firm texture and a shell that is not slippery. The color of the shell may vary from grayish-green to tan to light pink. If purchased cooked, the shell should be pink and the meat should be pink with red spots. A stale shrimp has an offensive ammonia odor.

LOBSTER Most people find one or two lobsters are sufficient, depending on size. However, since we live where they are abundant, friends, and I hate to admit my own husband, have been known to sit and eat and chat, chat and eat, until they have consumed up to 24. So go by appetites — or your budget. I normally allow one large or two small per person.

Lobsters should be lively and vigorous showing movement of the legs. After cooking, the shell should be bright red and have a fresh, pleasant odor. Look for hard heavy shells and tails that curl up under the lobster when it is picked up. Live lobsters are either green-brown or deep blue in color.

Do not store live lobster on ice or in fresh water. Cover with a damp cloth or layer of seaweed in refrigerator or other cool place for up to 12 hours. Cooked lobster may be kept up to 48 hours in the refrigerator, but no longer.

CRAB Like lobster, crab should be lively and vigorous when you buy them.

Do not store live crab on ice or in fresh water. Cover with a damp cloth or layer of seaweed in refrigerator, or other cool place, for up to 12 hours. Cooked crab may be kept up to 48 hours in the refrigerator, but no longer.

When transporting seafood, keep it well iced. A few hours in the trunk of a car can completely ruin many fish and spoil your barbecue.

IMITATORS

The marketplace today has been invaded by some imitation or "restructured" seafood products. The basic ingredient is still fish, but it has been changed, added to and is sometimes sold as something other than what it is.

It usually tastes good and is pleasing in texture, but the additives bother me, especially as these products do not normally have ingredients listed. MSG, sugar, sorbital, salt, chemical flavourings, coloring agents and extracts can be part of the product. Just be aware of what you buy.

SURIMI is the raw material for a variety of restructured fish products. It begins as the mechanically deboned flesh of various species of fish. After a series of processing steps, including repeated washings and strainings, with the addition of sugar, sorbital and salt, the result is a concentrated fish paste. The paste is frozen and later thawed to be restructured into simulated shellfish—crab, scallop, shrimp and most recently, lobster. The flavor comes from the addition of real shellfish, a shellfish extract or a chemical flavoring.

A good percentage of the surimi manufactured today is from pollock and haddock.

The nutritional value of the imitation seafood varies with each manufacturer and is determined by the type of fish and the amount of natural fish, if any, involved.

That raises the question, when is a scallop not a scallop? The Prince Edward Island Department of Fisheries tells us that with the arrival of "KAMABOKO" on the market, consumers can purchase seafood products which resemble scallops, even though they are not!

"Scallops" made from kamaboko consist of a white fish (often pollock), a coloring agent, flavoring extracts and several other ingredients. Some may include a percentage of real scallop meat. These materials are mixed to make a smooth white material and are then mechanically formed into the shape of scallops.

There is a way to tell these imitations from regular scallops. Kamaboko "scallops" are very regular in shape, a perfect circle over one inch in diameter and about a half inch thick. Sea Scallops are often thicker and irregular in shape.

As long as you realize you are not buying the real thing, the substitute is fine. It is misrepresentation that causes concern. However, you would be advised to cook Kamoboko in a grill basket rather than on a skewer.

GENERAL RULES FOR COOKING FISH

Fish stays moist when cooked quickly at a high temperature.

Tender-flesh fish, such as whitefish fillets or brook trout, should be cooked in a hinged basket or foil or it will fall apart.

Firm-flesh fish, such as salmon, shark, swordfish can be marinated then grilled on a rack directly over the coals.

Whole fish can be stuffed, wrapped in foil or cooked in wire baskets.

Fatty fish, such as mackerel, can be cooked directly on the grill and don't need basting. They will, however taste better if marinated and/ or basted for a brief time.

For best results use fish that is at least 1-inch thick. Thinner fish can be cooked in foil or rolled.

For a smokier flavor with an electric or gas barbecue, cook with hood down or partially down, keeping the temperature hot.

Thaw frozen fish completely so that it will cook evenly.

Oil racks and grill just before cooking.

Don't overcook fish.

POACHING Any fish can be poached on the barbecue simply by sealing it in foil. Butter or oil the foil, salt and pepper the fish and lay it on. A daub of butter, squeeze of lemon, sprinkle of white wine, or combinations will enhance flavor. Add herbs or vegetables to taste.

BAKING This is different from poaching in that you don't add liquid. Butter or oil foil, lay fish on it, butter top and seal in foil. This is the best way to cook stuffed fish or some types of fish with vegetables or lemon.

ESTIMATING COOKING TIME It is the thickness of fish that determines the length of cooking time. Measure raw fish at the thickest point after stuffing or rolling. Assuming you are cooking 4-5 inches (10-12 cm) from medium hot coals, allow 10 minutes per inch (2.5 cm) if the fish is on the grill or in a basket. Add 5 minutes if fish is wrapped in foil. Very cold fish may take longer than fish at room temperature.

Larger fish should be cooked about 8 inches (20 cm) from the coals so that the outside doesn't overcook before the inside is done.

Cooking time varies depending on temperatures of coals, condition of fuel, outside winds and distance of fish from coals. Therefore suggested cooking times are guides only. Seafood on the grill cooks quickly and is a hands-on operation.

CHECKING FOR DONENESS Fish is done when the flesh is opaque rather than transluscent, with no signs of pink near the backbone. A whole fish is cooked if juices run clear when flesh is pricked. Tug on one of the fins on the side; if it comes away easily the fish is cooked. Fish is done when it flakes easily when tested with a fork.

ADD ZIP For extra zip, season your fish with spices other than salt, such as basil, lemon pepper, garlic, dill, thyme or marjoram. Tarragon adds flavor to fish.

SIMPLICITY IS BEST

You will note as you read through this book that we have tried to stick to simple-to-prepare, nutritious recipes, suitable for casual outdoor eating. You will find no rich sauces, creamy dressings or complicated recipes. The butters, for example, are simply softened butter with herbs or other ingredients added. Fish or seafood is on the grill for such a short cooking time, that we have never found it necessary to clarify butter.

It is my opinion that barbecue or grill cooking should be simple, as enjoyable for the cook as well as for guests and it should be hands on. I like everyone to get involved.

GRILL 'N' CHAT

One of my fondest memories of good times past recalls evenings spent sitting around a fondue pot with friends. We'd cook a little, play a little, eat a bit more, and talk until we were pretty well hoarse.

The key to the good times is, of course, the fondue pot. Sitting around cooking morsels of food, is a perfect ice breaker, conversation starter or what have you. It bonds those present.

Fondues are in my mind a winter thing. A great way to pass an evening with friends, all snuggled in the warm, satisfying one of the primal urges—our appetites—while enjoying good conversation and lots of laughs.

In spring, summer and fall look to the barbecue, especially if you have a small table model or a hibachi to provide similar entertainment.

Some foods are meant to grill for a short time (like skewered shrimps or prawns), others are best cooked to personal taste. Some are a bit fiddly, like Grilled Clams Parmesan, others are fun, like mussels cooked on the grill and dipped straight into a pot of lemon butter, kept melted right there. You can even follow the fondue tradition of cooking your seafood then dipping it in a variety of sauces.

When looking for things for a grill 'n' chat session select those that don't take long to cook, take up little room on the grill and can be eaten simply with just a dipping sauce. Check out the sections on nibblers and skewered food.

What you need: aprons are a nice touch, fun and appreciated; skewers, tongs and hot mitts to go around; recipes to hand around that are simple (then folks know what they are doing); lots of plates and enthusiastic friends to enjoy it all.

EYE TEST FOR COOKED FISH

UNDERDONE: Fish that hasn't been cooked enough looks translucent.

JUST RIGHT: When opaque at its thickest part and the flakes lift apart but not too easily, fish is juicy and delicious.

OVERDONE: If you wait until fish flakes too easily, it could be dry and tasteless.

Generally you can plan on cooking 10 minutes per inch/2.5 cm thickness of fish. If the fish is less than 1 inch/2.5 cm thick, adjust cooking time downward accordingly. Add an extra 2 to 4 minutes if baking with sauce or cooking a stuffed fish. Double the cooking time if the fish is frozen.

HOW TO BUY FISH

FRESH: Look for firm-textured, moist, glossy flesh with no sign of dryness. Odor, if there is any, should be mild and fresh, never "fishy."

FROZEN: Look for tightly wrapped packages free of excessive ice crystals. Squeeze or press package — it should feel solid, with no airpockets or spaces. The fish itself should be free of ice crystals and have a fresh odor and clear color.

If you are going to prepare frozen fish with a coating, thaw first in refrigerator in original wrapping. Remove from the package and pat dry with paper towels. Cook the same day.

Never refreeze thawed or partially thawed fish, even after you've cooked it.

HOW TO STORE FISH

FRESH: Wrap loosely in waxed paper or foil; place in refrigerator; cook within 24 hours.

FROZEN: Store in freezer in original package from 3 months for fat fish (salmon, perch, bluefish, mackerel) to 6 months for lean fish (cod, flounder, sole).

Barbecues, Grills & Fires

I once read that the original barbecues were actually lamb roasts, reminiscent of the Hawaiian pig roasts where a pit was dug in the ground, and a fire built in it. In this instance the pig carcass lay on the coals covered with leaves.

The characteristic of a lamb roast is that a wooden frame supported the meat, usually a whole lamb (skinned, cleaned and split, I presume) over the hot coals. It took hours to cook and was, I am sure, delicious.

The word barbecue is derived from *barbacoa*, (American Spanish) meaning a framework of sticks. Food to be cooked was put on such a framework, often with sticks interwoven over the food and the occasion was probably a fiesta.

That same principle is followed by some outdoor lovers today who use portable racks to cook over coals from a campfire. Some woodstoves even come with such racks.

The essential items for today's barbecue have been modernized, and yet have stayed the same. We still use a rack, but have replaced the wood with metal which will last indefinitely if it is cleaned and stored properly.

We seldom use firewood today, opting instead for more portable charcoal or briquets, a modern propane gas-fired flame which heats lava or ceramic briquets or an electric grill.

My personal choice is hardwood charcoal and nobody is going to defer me from that. Food tastes better. However, the convenience of the propane or electric barbecue cannot be ignored. Because we prefer outdoor meals away from home, we have a portable propane barbecue and we have found it very useful.

TYPES OF BARBECUES

There are several types of grills or barbecues. Your purchase depends on where and how you will use your unit. Apartment dwellers cooking on a balcony, for example, are best with a gas barbecue simply because disposal of coals can be a problem. Electric counter-top units are ideal in winter. Those who entertain a lot at home may want a permanent charcoal-burning fireplace built, or invest in a large gas barbecue centre. Travellers will go for portable units. Think about where you are going to use it, and where you can store it.

Finish is important. Porcelain enamel finishes are best for both long life and easy care. Painted steel must be stored inside and cleaned after each use. Cast steel needs the same care but seems to last longer than painted steel which is thinner.

If you use your unit year-round invest in something durable (heavier or thicker body) and with a cover; they hold heat better in cold weather.

Being a purist of sorts I like to do things in the old ways so I prefer cooking with hardwood charcoal over all others. I can tell the difference in taste and I like the mental feeling of security and well-being that an open fire or charcoal grill gives me. My husband, on the other hand, likes the convenience of propane. Thus we have both. Our charcoal-burning units get abused rather badly as we lug them to the beach a lot. Sand is hard on them. Because of that we usually buy cheaper ones and get a new one every year or two. For that, I like the little ones with a lid which you can fill with charcoal and lighting cubes at home, pop in a garbage bag and take that way. It cuts down on stuff to carry.

BRAZIERS OR FREE-STANDING GRILLS Any uncovered barbecue, including hibachis, can be considered braziers. Some have half hoods, or covers which can hold a rotisserie. Normally they burn charcoal or briquets. You should look for adjustable grills to move food close to or further away from the heat source. They can be any shape.

Units with a fitted cover are probably the most useful because they can be used as a grill or brazier, or, with the cover on, you can cook larger items such as whole chickens or turkeys, roasts, even masses of baked potatoes. You can roast, steam, smoke and so on. The cover is great if it's wet or windy, to reduce cooking time, protect from spatters, and for winter cooking to help hold the heat. There should be a vent to allow air flow.

Portable units today meet every need. They even have one for a boat which has the burning bowl on a swinging gadget that keeps it level, even when dipping up and down in waves. Throw away units are great for cyclists, motorcyclists and hikers. Fireplace grills work well in woodstoves, and are especially useful during power failures.

GAS GRILLS These come in portable or full-sized units which use gas, such as propane, to heat up a bed of lava rock or ceramic briquets which then cook in the same way as the charcoal briquets. They are very convenient, easy to use, faster to be ready to cook on and "in style."

ELECTRIC COUNTER-TOP UNITS These are just coming on to the market. Designed for grilling indoors, they will be a great favorite during the winter. The secret to successful barbecuing is to buy a unit with large enough elements to provide a good heat.

WATER SMOKERS A recent addition to the barbecue market are smokers which keep food moist while slowly cooking with charcoal briquets and aromatic woods. There are both gas and electric units. Most have two pans, the bottom for coals, the top for water, then the food sits on a rack above. The food is steam-smoked for hours and does not need to be tended very often. Some have multi-levels of racks which are great for hunters or fishermen. Some smokers can also be used as grills by putting the charcoal pan under the rack and removing the top.

You will get good results if you follow the manufacturer's instructions with any of these types of barbecues. They built them, they know how they should be used. A few of our tips for operation follow:

CHARCOAL AND BRIQUETS

LIGHTING CHARCOAL OR BRIQUETS You don't need liquid fuel to start charcoal, but if you do use it, please read and follow the directions on the container. Never squirt the stuff on a fire that has already been lit, even if it doesn't appear to be going. I've seen a can of fuel catch fire when someone did that and it was only luck that averted a tragedy. The flame traveled up the gas faster than he could drop the can.

A safer fire starter can be found quite easily. You can buy commercial cubes to light with a match, or use shredded milk cartons and a small pile of wood kindling. Carefully mound charcoal or briquets around your starter in a shape like a tepee or pyramid, light and wait. You can also buy gadgets like chimney starters which use newspaper or electric starters for charcoal.

It is important that you start enough charcoal to provide a good bed of coals which will last through the whole cooking time. This takes some practise with the barbecue you have as all models tend to cook a little differently. Basically though you need 1 inch/2.5cm thickness of live coals for every 15 minutes of cooking time. Spread them out in the grill extending a little beyond the area of the food to be cooked, then mound to light.

Depending on weather and type of fuel used it will take ½ hour to 1½ hours to get the glowing coals you need for cooking. The fire will blaze up when first lit, but after a time it will calm down and red hot coals will be seen. You should never cook over live coals until they are covered with a light coating of gray ash. That signifies correct temperature. Spread the coals to the required thickness, piling the access to the side so that they can be raked in as more fire is needed. As I write this it all seems a bit complex, but it isn't and once you've done it, a sixth sense develops which helps you judge the right cooking temperatures and times.

COALS ARE READY During the day you can judge coals as ready when ALL coals are ashy grey. If some are still black, cooking will be uneven. At night they should be glowing red and kept that way by keeping them close together and shaking them up every so often to rid them of ash. Remember that the closer together coals are the hotter they will cook. To lower temperature spread them apart.

SQUIRT IT OUT Fats which drip onto red hot coals can cause flare-ups of flame which will burn food and leave an unpleasant taste. To put those flames out use a squirt bottle of water. We save a plastic detergent bottle, wash it well and fill with water. The kind with an adjustable spray works best. It is packed along with the barbecue when we travel. A more delicate method is to use a brush to sprinkle water over the flame.

GAS GRILLS

CONNECTING PROPANE Check all connections by applying a soapy solution to them. If bubbles appear when the gas is turned on, shut the unit off and reconnect or tighten joints until bubbles are no longer visible.

LIGHTING THE GAS BARBECUE Follow the instructions that come with your barbecue. A flint striker, or long fireplace matches, are best to light propane. You should also make sure the wind is not going to blow out the flame. It's a real problem for us because we live in a very windy area. We pop our portable into the back of our pickup truck (it has a cap) which has been positioned to eliminate the wind, and we never leave it unattended.

WHEN IT IS READY TO COOK While in theory you can light a gas grill and cook on it immediately, we always warm ours up for a while. We find the cooking is better once the lava rock or ceramic briquets are heated through. Sometimes fat left from a previous meal will cause smoke the first few minutes so we wait until it clears. To eliminate that as much as possible we let the gas burn for a while after we have finished cooking.

CLEANING THE GAS GRILL Follow the instructions which come with your barbecue for best results. To keep a gas or propane barbecue in safe working order it should be cleaned with hot soapy water or oven cleaner. If the burner needs cleaning, remove it and use a brush to clean a cast iron burner, or a cloth and soapy water to clean a stainless steel burner. A thin wire can be used to open any clogged burner parts. When you put it back, make sure it is seated properly at the gas valves. Don't tamper with the air shutter at the base of the burner without referring to the manual for instructions—I suggest giving it to a qualified person.

Lava briquets should be spaced in a single layer, and turned several times during the cooking season so that residues can burn off during cooking.

SHIELD FROM WIND If you find the wind is affecting either type of barbecue you can make a shield using foil and coathanger wire.

AROMATIC WOODS

The biggest news to hit the food scene in recent years is the use and availability of aromatic woods for the barbecue. In fact so strong has been the influence that American food is said to finally have found an identity, triggered by taste buds drooling over foods that have been smoked, grilled, and barbecued over natural woods or smoking chips.

Purists will turn to exotic woods like grapevine cuttings from France, but for most of us Mesquite and hickory are ideal. The later products are becoming readily available where barbecue supplies are sold. These products are packaged similar to charcoal and have suggested instructions on the packages.

CAMPFIRES

It must be said. You do not need fancy units which cost many hundreds of dollars to cook darn good barbecued food. They are fine if you want to go that route, but the most simple fire will do if prepared properly.

Just remember you cook over coals, not flames. Think back to those days as a Girl Guide or Boy Scout when delicious meals were cooked over an open fire. I can remember making 5-gallon oil cans into a charcoal stove and reflector oven and using tin cans for pots. We used to make firestarters from strips of birch bark, dried weed stalks and even roll strips of newspaper into "fire bugs" which were dipped into paraffin wax. These were made in advance and taken along on camping trips where we would feel so smug about getting our fire started before any of the other girls.

We learned several methods of fire-laying and building fireplaces, but the things that stuck stand me in good stead even today when I light the woodstove. I still place two large sticks parallel to each other, place papers, then kindling in the middle with larger pieces crossed across the top. This creates the right draft to get the fire going and will hold a good bed of coals. If you are outside you can lift one of the logs to get a good draft if needed.

The very best fires though were the Cowboy Keyhole which we used to make in my "cowboy and Indian" stage. Stones were laid in a keyhole shape and the main fire laid in the circle part. Hot coals were raked down into the narrow part of the keyhole, and a rack for cooking was placed over them. It was a primitive barbecue to be sure, but worked well and would boil a kettle in no time.

When cooking over a campfire it's important to remember that you need coals for broiling, grilling or barbecuing. Flames are OK for boiling, but will burn food cooked directly over them. You must be patient and prepare the right kind of fire for cooking over before you start.

CAMPFIRE COOKERY We are assuming that you are catching your own fish here and will have to prepare them yourself.

Trout are the easiest to prepare. Just scrape off the slime with your knife, open the belly, remove the entrails and blood up to the back bone, and they are ready.

SCALING is sometimes necessary. Lay the fish down flat on a surface you have sprinkled with salt. Now shake a bit of salt over the fish to keep it from slipping. Hold the fish firmly with one hand while scraping from tail to head with a knife, using either the back of your good knife, or a dull blade, and finally rinse the fish in clean water.

Some freshwater fish such as bass, perch and pickerel can be skinned rather than scaled. To do this cut off the fins, loosen the skin just behind the gills and pull it off using your knife and thumb to ease it down.

CLEANING is not as bad as it looks. Just hold the fish firmly in one hand (remember salt will stop it slipping). Insert a sharp knife at the vent (anal opening) and slit the belly up to the head. Free the gills then remove the entrails and blood up to the backbone, using your hand. Scrape out the belly, rinse briefly then wipe dry, inside and out. If you are squeamish about handling the entrails put your hand in a plastic bag or use a spoon.

FILLETING is preferred these days, although it is not as easy to barbecue fillets as whole fish. Slit the belly from vent to head and clean. Hold the fish by the head and make a knife cut across the fish, just below the gills. When the knife hits the backbone turn the blade flat, towards the tail. Draw the knife down the backbone, carefully loosening the fillet, until about an inch from the tail. Flip the fillet over, loosen it from the skin at the tail end and continue to draw your knife up until you have removed the fillet from the skin. Repeat on the other side of fish. Sometimes it is best to leave the skin on for grilling, especially in soft-flesh fish. Experienced old-timers usually don't bother to gut the fish before filleting, but I think beginners are best to do so.

HUNG TROUT This is for when you are out fishing and have a catch to cook but no utensils. Leaving the head in place, clean the trout and slit from just below the gills down to the vent. Remove the entrails, clean and fill the belly with butter. Then tie or sew the cavity closed; tieing under each set of gills with string works well. Hang the fish from a stick before a reflector fire (a fire built against a rock or in front of a metal reflector). When the butter oozes out the fish is done — and delicious.

PLANKED FISH This is good for large fish with thick fillets. Fasten the fillets, skin down, to a split log or plank (use wooden pegs or small nails) and cook before a reflector fire. The oil from the skin is usually enough to keep the fish from sticking to the wood but to be on the safe side, oil or butter the plank before placing the fish on it. It doesn't take long to cook so watch it! If the fish appears to be drying baste with butter.

Whitefish is nice "planked." Dot it with butter and cook until almost done, then sprinkle with paprika and continue cooking until it's a golden brown. Serve right from the plank.

FOILED FISH Cooking in foil is a simple way of preparing fish over a fire. If hiking you can fold some foil and tuck it into your pack very easily. Whole fish can be wrapped with a couple of slices of bacon or brushed with butter, then wrapped tightly in foil and placed on the top of the coals. Cooking time is 15-20 minutes for a whole fish. Fillets cooked the same way will be done in 10-15 minutes. Both are good if lemon slices are added, or juice squeezed over, or an onion sliced in with the fish.

HOW HOT IS IT Many recipes, even for barbecuing, call for knowledge of the temperature. Here is a good way to measure which becomes accurate with practice.

Hold your palm in front of a fire or over a grill and count out the time when you have to move your hand away. Put your hand where the food will go. Count slowly (use the one and one, two and two, method).

— A slow fire (250-325 degrees F) will give a 6 to 8 count
— A medium fire (325-400 degrees F) a 4 to 5 count
— A hot fire (400-450 degress F) a 2-3 count. Charcoal coals will be covered with a gray ash
— A very hot fire (over 450 degrees F) a one count. Charcoal or briquets should be glowing with some gray ash around the edges.

WINTER GRILLING

Barbecuing is especially enjoyable in the winter as long as you prepare for it. Hikers, crosscountry skiers, photographers, nature lovers and of course outdoor types just need to be motivated to try it once and they will be hooked! Here are a few tips which will make the experience more enjoyable.

— Brush the snow off the barbecue; it will reduce the internal cooking temperature if left to melt off. If it's snowing, try to have the barbecue sheltered by a porch roof, picnic shelter, overhang or open garage. **Never grill in closed places like a garage with the door closed. Carbon monoxide is deadly. Also stay away from anything flammable.**
— Turn the grill so that the wind is at the back. Not only will you protect the flame from going out, but you will also stop cold draughts from reducing the cooking temperature.
— Have everything ready before you start cooking. Food prepared, implements ready and serving plates at hand. Don't forget veggies and bread on the grill to go with your seafood.
— Be prepared to serve and eat right off the grill. Food cools too fast to be fancy. Seafood cooks fast so its ideal for the cook, who isn't forced to stand in the cold too long.
— Finish off the feast with a few toasted marshmallows and hot chocolate—right from the grill.
— . . . And dress warmly!

Utensils & Cooking Aids

None of the following are necessary to grill seafood; they just make the job easier and safer.

— long-handled tongs, the best have sides like egg flippers
— long-handled basting brush
— heavy-duty hot mitt
— water squirt-bottle
— wire baskets with handles at least 12 inches long
            — whole fish cooker
            — hinged grill baskets
— skewers (steel or bamboo) and a skewer holder
— flat spit basket or tumble basket for a rotisserie
— heavy-duty aluminum foil
— wire-brush for cleaning grill

Wire baskets are great for cooking seafood because it is held securely so that turning can be done without breaking the delicate flesh apart. The only way to cook fish on a rotisserie is with a basket, otherwise it falls apart. Tumble baskets only work for shellfish such as scallops and shrimps which must be constantly basted.

BARBECUE CART Setting up a cart with all of your supplies is a great plus for aficionados of barbecuing. You can load all the spices, utensils, plates and so on onto the cart and just wheel it over beside the barbecue. If you live out of doors in the summer the basics can be left right on the cart ready for next time. Pot holders and tools can hang from hooks, spices placed in carry trays and charcoal and starter fluid on the bottom shelf. Be sure to make or buy a sturdy cart.

HANGER A row of hooks to hang cooking utensils and a hot mitt keeps everything handy, and clean. It can be fitted to your barbecue or picnic table.

ALUMINUM FOIL—GRILLER'S BEST FRIEND

Aluminum foil is wonderful stuff for the barbecue devotée. Food can be poached or steamed in it; it catches drips, gathers up ashes, protects from the wind; it makes into pots and pans and protects food in transit.

Always use heavy-duty foil at the barbecue. The lighter weight must be doubled or it will rip.

WRAPPED COOKING Fragile fillets, whole fish, steaks all take kindly to being wrapped, as do vegetables. Basically, if you tightly wrap, allowing no steam to escape, you are either steaming or poaching fish.

The best, and strongest, method of wrapping is to lay food in the centre of foil large enough to allow for folding at the top and ends. Pull the sides up first, put them together and fold over several times to lock in the moisture. Then fold or roll in the ends so that you have a secure little package. This works best for whole fish.

The other popular type of wrapping is to bundle up the food. Lay food in centre of a square, pull the corners up and close all seams by rolling and pressing closed. This works best for shellfish, or rolled fillets.

Vegetables with thin skin, like corn or potatoes can be wrapped in foil to prevent charring while cooking .

PREVENTS BURNING If you have a fish that is very thick through, the tail section may burn before the rest cooks. Cover the tail with foil, just as you would the end of drumsticks on a turkey or the bones on a rack of lamb.

BARBECUE LINER Line the barbecue bowl with foil before placing charcoal or briquets in. Light and cook in the usual way. Once the coals have cooled, roll the ashes up in the foil and discard. You will extend the life of the barbecue, make cleanup easier and get maximum heat from your coals.

DRIP CATCHER Fat dripping down into coals can make a mess and cause flare-ups. Make a foil bowl to catch fat. Place it over the coals, or, if you have a unit with a drain in the bottom, under the barbecue.

WARMER Our barbecues are small so we usually cook potatoes and such before fish which takes just a few minutes. We take the cooked potatoes, still in foil, place them in another sheet of foil, wrap lightly and push under the barbecue where there is some heat.

BARBECUE COVER If you don't have a cover for your barbecue and want one, you can make one out of a few strips of foil, tucked carefully around the grill (use oven mitts). The one time I bless this method is when I want to bake a lot of potatoes. By sealing them in with a layer of foil they cook more quickly and evenly. Tightly seal this cover at the back and loosely at the front, then you can carefully lift it to check underneath. You can also make a frame of wire or coathangers for a cover that will lift off easily.

WIND SHIELD If you find your self stuck in the wind with a barbecue that either blows out (gas) or won't cook properly because of wind, build a shield. In the case of propane blowing out, you can wrap the bottom on the wind side to give protection to the flame. The top is a little more difficult; you need a frame covered with foil. Wire or old coathangers hooding half of the grill and covered with foil does an admirable job.

PREPARING THE GRILL

— Before barbecuing make sure you have plenty of gas in the tank or charcoal on hand.
— Always preheat the barbecue.
— Lightly brush hot rack with oil just before cooking to discourage food from sticking OR spray with vegetable shortening before placing on the barbecue.
— Clean the grill with a wire brush after each use.
— Season rack by oiling regularly.

Marinating

Barbecues, fish and marinades belong together, for this is how you enhance flavors to make them irresistible. The marinade is also a cooking aid, keeping fish moist and tender in the simplest possible way. Marinades are a mixture of liquids and seasonings.

Generally you can marinate any type of fish, but the leaner the fish, the shorter the marinating time. The flesh of lean fish is already tender and a long marinating time will cause it to break apart too easily.

The marinade can be prepared ahead and kept in a cool place for up to 3 days, unless the recipe says otherwise. They are best used at room temperature, but use common sense in hot weather.

Mix marinade ingredients together in a container suitable for storage if preparing ahead, or in a bowl, shallow dish or jar which will hold fish and marinade. If we are barbecuing away from home, I mix marinades in a large mason jar before we leave home, screwing the top on tight to transport in the cooler. Then I add seafood to the jar when it is time to marinate. Another good method is to place marinade and seafood into a heavy-weight plastic bag. Close securely then lay in a bowl or second bag (in case of leaks). Turn the bag several times during marinating. I never use anything but glass, ceramic or plastic containers for marinades because the acidic content can cause a flavor exchange from metals.

Before marinating unskinned whole fish, slash two or three times per side, cutting slits about 1/2 inch (1 cm) deep. This allows flavor to penetrate fish.

Remember, the longer a fish marinates, the more flavor it absorbs. Lean, delicate fleshed fish absorbs a strongly flavored marinade in about 15 minutes; milder flavors need about an hour.

Don't marinate delicate-flesh fish for longer than 15 minutes in lemon or lime juice based marinades. The acid in the juice can "cook" the fish.

Reserve marinade for basting. Marinades do keep seafood moist while cooking. For best results try to brush a marinade on two or three times while grilling.

Marinated fish is excellent wrapped in foil with some of the marinade and cooked over the grill. You can pierce the foil to allow a smoke flavor to penetrate fish, but you will lose some of the marinade. Be careful lifting it off the grill—drips will be hot.

Allow 1/3 to 1/2 cup (79-118 mL) marinade for each pound (454 g) of fish. Discard any leftover marinade.

Preparing marinades can seem a fiddly job what with chopping fresh herbs, garlic, ginger and so on. We solved that problem with the acquisition of a mini-chopper, a small electric appliance that chops half a cup or so at a time. I just put in cloves of garlic, pieces of ginger, zest of citrus skin, fresh herbs, onion and even mushrooms. It minces, rather than chops, but I find this wonderful for marinades as flavors blend very well and large chunks of ingredients do not burn on my seafood.

Recipes using marinades for enhancing flavor are found throughout the book. For a complete listing of marinades refer to the index, under marinades. Please remember that all marinades can be used for numerous "cuts" and types of seafood. Recommended use is found with the recipe.

Fish Fillets

F illets, the meaty sides of fish cut lengthwise from the backbone, are generally the most popular form of fish as they are easy to handle, freeze and package well, and have most of the bones removed. Fillets, however, are fragile and should either be cooked in a grilling rack or in foil, and with great care. Those with the skin left on one side (usually mackerel or other fatty fish) can be cooked directly on the grill with care. Generally count on 3-4 servings from 1 pound (454g) of fillets.

Grilled Fish with Butter Topper

fish fillets, use fairly firm fleshed fillets
vegetable oil or cooking oil spray

Tarragon Garlic Butter OR your favourite herb butter

This is where you will really value a flat hinged grill. Spray grill with an oil cooking spray or brush with vegetable oil. Lightly brush fish with oil or butter, place in grill and close it tightly, secured with a twist tie if necessary.

Place over the hot coals and cook until fish flakes. Frequently baste with oil or butter.

Just before removing from the grill, top with Tarragon Garlic Butter and swiftly place on serving plates. Delicious.

Greek Oregano Grill

I always visualize Greek fishermen cooking this type of dish at waterside as the sun sets, probably wrongly, but it's a nice image. While we prefer it for fatty fish like mackerel, lean fish also take this flavor well.

8 small or 4 large mackerel fillets, skins on

Greek Oregano Marinade:
1/2 cup olive oil *118mL*
1/4 cup fresh lemon juice *59mL*
1 tbsp zest of lemon, minced *15mL*

2 tsp fresh oregano, minced *10mL* or 1 tsp dried oregano *5mL*
1 tsp minced garlic *5mL*
1/2 small red onion, sliced very thin or finely chopped to make 1/2 cup *118mL*

Mix all marinade ingredients until well blended. Marinate fish for about 30 minutes. Lay flesh side down on grill and cook 4 minutes, baste, then turn and cook 4-5 minutes more, basting twice. Serves 4

Bluefish with spicy Yogurt Marinade

This combination of flavors is best suited for fatty fish such as bluefish or mackerel. Because of the yogurt it is best cooked in foil, however I have placed fillets in a hinged basket and basted while grilling. It tasted great but was a bit messy.

1 lb bluefish fillets (or any fatty fish) *454g*

Spicy Yogurt Marinade:
1 tsp ground coriander seeds *5mL*
1/2 tsp ground cumin *2.5mL*

1/4 tsp ground turmeric *1.25mL*
1/4 tsp ground red pepper *1.25mL*
1 cup plain low-fat yogurt *236 mL*

Prepare marinade by putting spices in a small, preferably non-stick skillet over medium heat. Stir about 2 minutes to bring out flavors. Cool 1 minute then add the yogurt and stir until well blended. Marinate fish for 30-60 minutes. Spoon marinade over foil where fish will lie. Place fish on foil and top with another spoonful of marinade. I usually roll the fillets or place one on top of another, allowing 10 minutes per inch (2.5 cm) of thickness cooking time. Seal foil and cook on grill. If grilling over the coals, baste with marinade during cooking.

Simplest Fillets

Place fish fillets, cod or any lean fish, on heavy-duty aluminum foil which has been lightly brushed with butter or margarine. Sprinkle with salt, lemon pepper and a small amount of minced onion. If desired, the fillets may be topped with mashed potatoes, tomato slices or lemon slices. Dot with butter or margarine. Wrap the foil tightly and seal the edges. Place on a hot grill for 10-20 minutes, depending on thickness.

Great for busy homemakers who want dinner in a hurry. Put the fish on and prepare a salad while it's cooking. Use your imagination and make a packet for each person. If you have fussy eaters this recipe makes life simpler.

Oriental Fillets

Good for all types of fish, fat or lean, fillets, steaks or whole.

1-1½ pounds fish fillets or steaks
    454-681g

Ginger Soy Marinade:
1/3 cup vegetable oil 79mL
1/3 cup soy sauce *79mL*
1/4 cup thinly sliced green onion
    59mL
2 tbsp grated fresh ginger root
    30mL

1½ tbsp rice-wine vinegar
    22.5mL
1 small clove garlic, minced
1 tsp jalapeno pepper (optional)
    5mL
1 tsp sesame oil *5mL*

Mix all marinade ingredients to blend well. Marinate fish about 15 minutes. Baste with marinade while cooking in a hinged grill basket.

Cheesey Rolled Sole

1 lb sole fillets (4 fillets) *454g*
1 pkg (4 oz) cream cheese *114g*
1 tbsp lemon juice *15mL*

dash each of salt and pepper
marjoram (to taste)
fresh spinach paprika

Spread cheese over fillets. Season to taste with marjoram, salt and pepper. Cover with one spinach leaf on each fillet. Roll up like a jelly roll. Place on heavy-duty aluminum foil. Sprinkle with paprika. Seal packages by making double fold. Cook about 4 inches above hot coals. Allow 10 minutes per inch (2.5 cm) of thickness of rolled fish. Serves 4

Sole Roll-ups

When you can get thin fillets of white fish such as sole, they are nice rolled as they keep their moistness. Either cook in a hinged grill basket or in foil.

4 large sole fillets	4 thin slices of fine ham
4 cooked whole asparagus spears (canned are fine)	herb or garlic butter (see p 87)

Spread herb or garlic on sole fillets; lay slice of ham on each, then roll each around an asparagus spear. Use string or a skewer to hold roll together and place in hinged grill basket. Grill over medium-hot coals, turning only once, basting several times with herb or garlic butter. Serves 2

Simple Orange Sole

4 good size sole fillets (or other white fish)	Orange Butter (see p 88)
1-2 oranges	lemon or orange pepper

Oil hinged wire grill and place sole fillets in it after rubbing them with orange butter and sprinkling with seasoned pepper. Cook over hot grill, squeezing orange juice over each side during cooking. Be sure they don't dry, using Orange Butter to baste if necessary.

For a meal with a Caribbean accent serve Orange Sole with grilled fruit, such as Rum Soaked Oranges or Coconut Peaches (see index).

Tangy Dill Fillets

A dill sauce can be used on the barbecue or under the broiler with shark, swordfish, mackerel or any other strong-flavored fish. Dill is a favorite with fish; combined with horseradish and onion it has a tongue-tingling zip, pleasing to many palates.

fish fillets or steaks	1 tbsp horseradish sauce *15mL*
Tangy Dill Sauce:	2 tbsp chopped onion *30mL*
1 tbsp lemon juice *15mL*	1/2 tsp dill weed *2.5mL*

Mix all ingredients then use to baste fish while grilling.

Fishburgers

1 lb fish fillets, remove bones
   454g
4 kaiser or hamburg buns
alfalfa sprouts or lettuce
sliced tomato

Barbecue Marinade:
1/2 cup barbecue sauce *118mL*
2 tbsp vegetable oil *30mL*
1 tsp basil *5mL*

or

Burger Marinade:
1/4 cup vegetable oil *59mL*
1 tbsp lemon juice *15mL*
2 tbsp ketchup *30mL*
1/2 tsp Worcestershire sauce
   2.5mL
1 tbsp minced onion *15mL*

Mix marinade ingredients, then marinate fillets for 30 minutes. Cook in an oiled hinged grill basket, turning once and basting with reserved sauce. Wrap 4 buns with foil and heat 3-5 minutes on the barbecue or split the buns and toast over coals. Top each bun with fish fillet, alfalfa sprouts and tomato slices. Add dressing if desired and put lid on bun. Makes 4 fish burgers.

Bannock on a Stick — An Old Indian Recipe

One summer I decided to indulge myself by taking a course in folk history at the University of Prince Edward Island. Our instructor, sly devil that he was, decided that the study of food and its preparation was part of the course and determined that three students should bring food each week. The class snacked, we all had fun and we got some great old recipes from days past.

This is an old recipe for bannock which was wrapped around a stick and cooked in the coals. The person who brought it to class stuffed each piece of bannock with fruit (raspberries and blueberries) before cooking . . . delicious. I tried wrapping dough around tuna and salmon salad mixtures . . . also delicious. I suggest a couple of practice runs to get this down pat.

1½ cup flour *354 mL*
1/2 tsp salt *2.5 mL*
1/2 cup water (or milk) *118 mL*

2 tsp baking powder *10 mL*
2 tbsp lard *30 mL*
filling of your choice for centre (if
   desired)

Combine, shape bannock then wrap around sticks. Rub with lard and cook in coals. Or shape into a rectangle, spread fruit or other filling down the middle, fold in sides and rub with lard. Cook on foil in a closed barbecue (cover down).

Monkfish with Mandarins

2 lb monkfish fillets (or cod,
    Boston bluefish, cusk, ocean
    perch, silver hake, catfish,
    dogfish, or halibut) *908 g*

Orange Sauce Marinade:
1/3 cup orange juice concentrate
    or orange juice *79 mL*

1/3 cup orange marmalade
    79 mL
2 tsp curry powder *10 mL*
1 can (10 oz) mandarins *300 mL*
1/3 cup mandarin juice *79 mL*

Mix marinade ingredients well, setting aside the mandarins. Allow marinade to blend for one hour then add fillets and marinate for 30 minutes. Place fillets in oiled hinged grill basket and grill 4 minutes on each side, basting several times with leftover marinade. Top each fillet with mandarins and cook for a minute longer to heat mandarins through.

Note: Topping fillets with mandarins is a bit fiddly in a grill basket. Mine is a flat rectangle so I carefully open it, place mandarins on and hold it carefully for the few seconds needed to heat them. Serves 4

Northern Woods Catfish

The hint of maple in this dish brings to mind a campsite beside a lake, bacon and fish sizzling in the cool crisp air. Delicious with bannock on a stick (recipe follows). The fish recipes comes to us from Nova Scotia and the bannock from Prince Edward Island.

1½ lb. maple flavor bacon *681g*
2 lb catfish fillets *1 kg*
1/2 cup melted butter *118 mL*

1/4 cup lime or lemon juice
    59 mL
1 tsp tarragon *5 mL*

Cover one side of a hinged grill basket with strips of bacon. Overlap horizontal edges because they will shrink during cooking. Place the fillets on the bacon and cover with remaining slices of bacon. Mix butter, juice and seasonings. Baste fillets with butter mixture while cooking. Turn frequently. Bacon should be crisp when fish is cooked. Serves 4

Blackened Shad

Shad, a member of the herring family, is very boney and for that reason is best filleted. It can be planked (see p 37), grilled or cooked by the following method for delicious outdoor eating. If you come across any roe, fry them up with bacon or butter. We found this recipe in an issue of *Food and Wine Magazine* which attributed it to Chef Paul Prudhomme who prepares blackened redfish at his New Orleans restaurant, K-Paul's. The secret to success is high heat, a cast-iron skillet and a tolerance for smoke. If your barbecue will not give you a high heat look for another heat source that will, without going indoors (because of the smoke).

1 ½ tsp coarse (kosher) salt *7.5 mL*   1 shad fillet (about 3/4 lb *340 g*)

Sprinkle a large well-seasoned cast-iron skillet with the salt and place it over a high heat for 10 minutes. Cut the shad fillet in half crosswise and place the pieces, skin-side down, in the pan. Cook over high heat, without turning or moving, for 6 minutes. Turn and cook the other side for 10 seconds. Serve the shad, blackened side up, as a main course with baked potatoes or potato salad.

Japanese Style Fillets and Veggies

1 lb cusk fillets (or any white fish) *454 g*
green pepper, zucchini, onion and mushrooms in bite-size pieces
cooked rice

1/2 cup white wine or seafood broth *118 mL*
1 tsp sugar *5 mL*
1/2 tsp ginger *2.5 mL*
1 clove garlic, minced
few drops Tabasco sauce

Japanese Marinade:
1/4 cup soya sauce *59 mL*

Mix marinade ingredients. Place fish fillets and variety of vegetables in foil. Spoon marinade over then seal foil by double folds. Cook 10-15 minutes over hot coals before checking for doneness. To serve place fish beside a bed of rice then pour vegetables and juice over rice.
Note: This marinade is also excellent for separately cooking vegetables in foil.

Fish Grilled in Lettuce Leaves

The lettuce leaves protect the fish, hold in the marinade, and char slightly, providing a smokey flavor in addition to being eminently edible. The wet tea leaves dampen down the fire a bit and emit an aromatic smoke.

I clipped this from a magazine several years ago and have often used it to wow visitors.

6 fish fillets or steaks (cod, halibut or salmon) about 6 oz/180 g each

12 dark-green outer leaves of romaine, escarole or other leaf lettuce

1½ tbsp vegetable oil *22.5 mL*

1 tbsp chopped fresh parsley *15 mL*

1 tbsp snipped chives or green onions *15 mL*

3 tbsp wet tea leaves (regular orange pekoe or other preferred aromatic tea) *45 mL*

Fennel Marinade:

1/3 cup lemon juice *79 mL*

1/3 cup olive or vegetable oil *79 mL*

1/4 cup soy sauce (optional) *59 mL*

2 tbsp chopped fresh parsley *30 mL*

2 tbsp snipped chives or green onions *30 mL*

1/2 tsp dried fennel leaves *2.5 mL*

Prepare marinade by mixing in a shallow dish. Add fish, turning to coat both sides. Marinate 1 hour at room temperature, turning several times. Heat up barbecue coals. Cut 12 pieces of kitchen twine long enough to tie around fish. To assemble each packet, lay 1 piece of twine lengthwise on work surface and another piece crosswise. Place 1 lettuce leaf on strings, top with a fish steak and spoon on some marinade with a few fennel seeds; sprinkle with some of the remaining parsley and chives. Cover with another lettuce leaf. Bring up the strings and tie. Brush packet with oil.

Sprinkle tea leaves over coals to cool them to a medium heat. Arrange packets on grill, top side up. Cook, 14 to 16 minutes, with the hood down (or lay a piece of foil over), turning half way through. Lettuce should be evenly charred with a fair amount of green showing. Test by opening one packet and checking that the fish is opaque and flakes easily. If not done, just re-wrap lettuce around fish and return to grill. Serves 6

Zesty Catfish Fillets

2 lb catfish fillets *908 g*

Zesty Marinade:
1/2 cup catsup, chili sauce or
    tomato sauce *118 mL*

1 small onion, minced 1 small
    garlic clove, finely minced
1/4 cup water *59 mL*
3 tsp prepared mustard *15 mL*
dash hot pepper sauce

Combine marinade ingredients in a saucepan and simmer, stirring frequently for 5-10 minutes or until well blended. Marinate fillets in sauce and refrigerate for at least 30 minutes, turning once or twice and brushing both sides with sauce. Remove fillets and arrange on a well-greased hinged grill basket. Cook over hot coals for 4 minutes on each side or until flesh flakes easily when tested with a fork. Use remaining marinade for basting during cooking.

Fish Steaks

F ish steaks, cross section slices of fish are excellent for barbecuing
as long as they are not cut too thin. I like them 3/4-1 inch (1.9-
2.5 cm) in thickness for best barbecuing. If a fish is more fatty than
usual it will show in the belly area, the small flaps of skin at the
bottom of the steak. They can be removed after cooking if desired.
Don't try to remove the skin before cooking as it holds the meat
together very efficiently. Allow 1 pound (454 g) for 2-3 servings.

Mexican Grilled Steaks

A hot pepper and lime juice marinade gives this a Mexican flavor.
Decrease the amount of chili pepper if you can't take the heat. Use
with any fish — fat or lean.

2 good sized fish steaks

Mexican Marinade:
1/3 cup fresh lime juice *79mL*
zest of 1 lime
3 tbsp vegetable oil *45mL*

1 medium, fresh jalapeno chili
pepper, seeded and minced to
make about 1 1/2 tbsp/*22.5mL*
or substitute a fresh serrano or 1
tsp crushed red pepper *5mL*

Mix marinade until well blended. Marinate fish for about 15 minutes
then grill basting with leftover marinade.

Salmon Steaks with Dill Vinaigrette

Serve with grilled cherry tomatoes, basted with the same sauce. Garnish with lemon.

4 salmon steaks, about 1 inch/ 2.5cm thick (6 oz/ *180g each*)

Dill Basting Sauce:
1/3 cup olive oil *79mL*
1/4 cup freshly squeezed lemon juice *59mL*
1 tbsp snipped fresh dill *15mL*

or 1 tsp dried dillweed *5mL*
1 tsp minced garlic *5mL*
1/2 tsp salt *2.5mL*
1/4 tsp freshly ground pepper *1.25mL*
1/4 tsp Dijon mustard *1.25mL*

Whisk sauce ingredients in a small bowl. Cover and let stand at room temperature at least 2 hours, or refrigerate up to 24 hours, to allow flavors to develop.

Place fish directly on lightly oiled grill, 4-6 inches (10-15 cm) above hot coals. Cook 8 to 10 minutes, turning once and brushing twice with sauce. Steaks are done when thickest part is barely opaque. Test with a fork. Serves 4

Note: Recipe makes 3/4 cup/177mL basting sauce. Pour about 1/4 cup/59mL into a bowl for use with the fish. Refrigerate remainder to use as a salad dressing or to baste grilled vegetables.

Hint: We really like this recipe but prefer more dill so we increased amount a little and marinated the steaks in the sauce for 1 hour. We made up kebabs of mushrooms, green pepper, onion and cherry tomatoes and basted them with the sauce, to serve with the steaks.

Baja Tuna with Salsa

Tuna steaks
Olive oil

Citrus Salsa (see index)

Preheat coals till hot, or a high grill. Rub olive oil into tuna steaks then grill until just opaque in the centre. Serve with Citrus Salsa.

Fish Steaks with Cucumber Sauce

So simple no one will believe it

4 fish steaks, such as halibut or
    salmon
1/4 cup bottled Creamy
    Cucumber prepared dressing
    59mL
2 green onions including tops,
    thinly sliced

2 tbsp chopped fresh dill weed
    30mL
or 1/2 tsp dried dill weed 2.5mL
salt and white pepper, to taste
1 lemon

Lightly oil both sides of the fish and place on the grill about 4 inches/
10cm from hot coals. Cook about 6 minutes.

Combine the dressing with the onions and seasonings. Turn steaks,
then top each one with a spoonful of the dressing. Leave as is until
fish is cooked and dressing is heated through. Serve with a lemon
wedge to squeeze over the top. Serves 4

Grilled Swordfish

2 swordfish steaks

Shallot/White Wine
    Marinade:
1/3 cup olive oil 79mL
2 tbsp dry white wine 30mL

1 tsp lemon juice 5mL
1 tbsp minced shallot 15mL
1 tbsp chopped fresh basil 15mL
pepper, to taste

In a small bowl whisk together oil, wine and lemon juice, then stir in
shallot, basil and pepper. Marinate fish no longer than 30 minutes.
Use remaining marinade to baste fish while grilling.

Curried Halibut

halibut steaks, 3/4 inch/2cm
    thick
lemon, zest the peel and juice
1/4 tsp curry powder 1.25mL

1/4 cup olive oil 59mL
1 tsp paprika 5mL
1 tsp finely chopped parsley
    5mL

Mix last five ingredients together to make the marinade. Place fish in
mixture for an hour, turning at least once. Grill fish in a hinged rack
basting with marinade several times during cooking. This cooks fairly
quickly, 4-5 minutes, so be careful it doesn't dry or overcook.

Mushroom/Almond Salmon Steaks

4 large salmon steaks
vegetable oil
1 lemon—cut one half into 4
    wedges, grate the rind from
    the other half and use juice in
    cooking

2 tbsp butter, softened *30mL*
1/4 lb chopped mushrooms
    113g
2 tbsp chopped parsley *30mL*
2 tbsp almond slivers *30mL*

Lightly oil steaks, sprinkle with lemon juice, and grill. While cooking, prepare topping by combining butter with grated lemon rind, mushrooms, parsley and almonds. Turn steaks then top with butter mixture, dividing between the 4 steaks. Cook until fish is done, then carefully remove to hot plates to serve with lemon wedges.

Fresh Tuna Piquant

6 8 oz tuna steaks 3/4 to 1 inch
    thick/6 *227g* steaks *2-2.5cm*
    thick

Split pepper marinade:
1/4 cup olive oil *59mL*
2 tbsp fresh lemon juice *30mL*

4 fresh oregano sprigs
4 whole black peppers (whole
    peppers run through a mini
    chopper are best, or freshly
    grind)

Piquant Sauce (see index)

Lay tuna in a shallow pan on top of 2 of the oregano sprigs. Drizzle on the olive oil, lemon juice, and pepper, turning steaks to cover both sides. Cover with remaining oregano. Cook about 4 minutes per side over medium high coals. To serve, top with Piquant Sauce.

Grouper Steaks with Lemon

6 grouper steaks, about 8 oz/
    227g each (excellent
    substitutes are halibut,
    whitefish, tile, or salmon)
1 tsp salt *5mL*

1/2 tsp pepper *2.5mL*
juice of 2 lemons
zest of 1 lemon
1/4 cup chopped fresh parsley
    59mL

Arrange steaks in a single layer in a shallow dish and sprinkle with other ingredients. Turn several times until steaks are well coated, then let sit about 30 minutes, longer if in refrigerator. Cook over a hot grill about 5 minutes on each side.

California Style Fish Grill

This is good made with swordfish, mackerel, shark, catfish, monkfish, as well as other firm-flesh steaks

2 lbs fish steaks *908 g*

Orange/Marjoram Marinade:
1/2 cup orange juice *118mL*
2 tbsp orange rind *30mL*
1/2 cup vegetable oil *118mL*
1/4 tsp marjoram *1.25mL*
1 tbsp chopped green onion
     15mL
dash pepper

Citrus Sauce:
1 cup chicken bouillon *236mL*
1 tsp cornstarch *5mL*
2 tbsp orange rind *30mL*
1/2 cup orange juice *118mL*
1 tbsp lemon juice *15mL*
1 orange, sliced

Mix together marinade ingredients. Pour over fish, and marinate for at least one hour.

Prepare Citrus Sauce while fish is marinating. Heat bouillon in a small saucepan. Mix cornstarch with orange juice and blend into bouillon. Add remaining ingredients and stir until sauce thickens. Sauce can be kept warm on the back of the barbecue. Serve with orange slices.

Remove fish from marinade and grill for 5-7 minutes on each side, depending on thickness. Baste with leftover marinade from time to time. Serve with a small amount of Citrus Sauce and an orange slice.

Saucy Italian Shark

2 lb shark steaks (or swordfish)
     908g
7½ oz tomato sauce *225mL*
1 tsp horseradish *5mL*
1/2 tsp salt *2.5mL*

1/2 tsp oregano *2.5mL*
1 cup sour cream *236mL*
1 tbsp chopped chives *15mL*

Combine tomato sauce, horseradish, salt and oregano. Reserve at least half of the sauce mixture to add to the sour cream. Brush fish with the mixture while fish is cooking over a hot grill. Meanwhile mix the remaining tomato sauce and sour cream in a heat-resistant dish and place on the grill to heat while the steaks cook. Serve by pouring sauce mixture over steaks and topping with chopped chives. Serves 4

Italian Balsamic/Basil Grill

Balsamic Vinegar comes to us from Italy and can be hard to find. Check out the specialty or Italian shops. Splash some over a salad made with black olives to accompany this fish. This marinade works very well for fatty fish, yet is not too overpowering for lean fish. Just shorten marinating time to 15 minutes for delicate-flesh fish.

2 fish steaks (butterfish, swordfish, tuna or bluefish)

Balsamic-Vinegar & Basil Marinade:
1/3 cup olive oil *79mL*
2 tbsp balsamic vinegar *30mL*
2 tbsp fresh basil, minced *30mL*

or 1 tsp dried basil *5mL*
1 tbsp fresh parsley, minced *15mL*
1 tbsp minced shallot *15mL*
pinch salt (optional)
1/8 tsp black pepper *.63mL*

Mix marinade ingredients well. Marinate fish for 30 minutes and use remaining marinade for basting. Serves 2

Tarragon Tuna

The wonderful herbed vinegars which are so popular today can form the base for marinades for fatty fish. They make preparation quick and easy. I love this marinade on shark, served with crusty Italian rolls, a salad and cantaloupe wedges sprinkled with snipped fresh tarragon. The fresh herb is a bonus; don't hesitate to use this marinade without it.

4 tuna steaks (or shark, swordfish or halibut)

Herbal Vinegar Marinade:
3 tbsp olive oil *45mL*
2 cloves garlic, minced

2 tbsp tarragon vinegar *30mL*
4-5 small leaves fresh tarragon, minced (optional)
black pepper

Mix marinade ingredients together and marinate fish 30-60 minutes. Grill over hot coals, frequently basting with leftover marinade. This is tasty served with a garlic or tarragon butter.

Whole Fish

The barbecue is ideal for cooking many species of fish whole. Directly on the grill, in a grill basket, in a flat spit basket, on your rotisserie or wrapped in foil, all work equally well. The fish can be stuffed or not but it must be cleaned and scaled. It will need to be moistened with a marinade, melted butter or oil during cooking or else wrapped in foil so that it is steamed or poached.

WHOLE FISH ON THE ROTISSERIE

Use preferred recipes for stuffing, marinades and basters. Oil a flat spit basket with vegetable oil or a non-stick cooking spray. Lay the fish in and close the basket securely, without squashing the fish. Follow directions that came with your rotisserie for centering the basket over medium hot coals. Turn on the rotisserie and baste fish as needed during cooking. Open gently so as not to break cooked fish.

WHOLE FISH ON THE GRILL

The problem with cooking whole fish on the grill is turning them and taking them off without breaking them up. Oiling the grill, and the fish itself, helps but the key to successfully cooking whole fish is to use a hinged wire fish basket. If you don't have one, try wrapping two strips of triple thickness foil around the fish and twisting it at the backbone to make little handles. The handles can be used to flip the fish over and then ease it onto a plate when cooked. Remember to baste while cooking to keep fish moist and prevent it from sticking.

Bacon Wrapped Trout

The bacon keeps the flesh from burning and gives it a wonderful flavor, especially if you use smoked bacon.

trout	lemon pepper
bacon	salt (optional)
lemon	

Clean trout well then rub the outside with lemon. Squeeze the remaining juice into the cavity and sprinkle with lemon pepper and salt if desired. Wrap the trout with bacon slices to cover. You may find it easier to use skewers or toothpicks to secure the bacon. Place fish on grill, and cook for 4-10 minutes depending on thickness of fish. Only turn once in cooking as bacon may become brittle.

Lemon Rice Haddock

Imagine a fish, fresh from the chilly waters of the Atlantic, cooked to perfection over the coals.

1 whole haddock, cod, salmon or trout (3-8 pounds/ *1.4-3.6 kg),* cleaned & scaled	1/4 cup lemon juice *59mL* 2½ cups water *625mL* 1 ¼ cups long grain white rice *295mL*
6 tbsp softened butter, *90mL*	
2 tbsp melted butter *30mL*	1-2 cups sliced mushrooms *236-472mL*
1 cup sliced celery *236mL*	
1 small onion, chopped 1/4 tsp basil *1.25mL*	1 tsp salt *5mL* 1/8 tsp pepper *.63mL*
2 tsp grated lemon peel *10mL*	1 small thin-skinned grapefruit, thinly sliced

Sauté celery and onion in 3 tbsp of the butter until tender. Add basil, lemon peel, lemon juice and water. Bring to a boil and add rice. Cover and reduce heat to low. Cook for 20 minutes, until rice is cooked.

Melt 3 tbsp/45mL of butter in a small skillet, add mushrooms and cook until tender. Mix with rice mixture. Season with salt and pepper. Place stuffing in fish.

Place half of the grapefruit slices on one side of a barbecue hinged fish basket. Place stuffed fish on top and cover with remaining grapefruit slices. Baste fish with melted butter while barbecuing. Allow the usual 10 minutes per inch (2.5 cm) of thickness (measure stuffed fish) for cooking. Turn at least once. Serves 4-6

Tasty Trout

1 large or 2 small trout. If frozen, defrost

Trout Marinade:
1/2 cup butter, melted *118mL*
1/4 cup chopped parsley *59mL*
2 tbsp catsup *30mL*

2 tbsp white vinegar *30mL*
2 cloves garlic, minced 2 tsp basil *10mL*
1 tsp salt *5mL*
1/4 tsp pepper *1.25mL*

Wash trout with cold water then pat dry with paper towel. Place fish in a shallow pan. Prepare the marinade by stirring other ingredients into the melted butter. Pour marinade over the trout, brushing so that it is completely covered. Marinade 30 minutes, turning trout several times. Place trout in an oiled hinged fish basket and grill over medium hot coals. Sear one side and turn to finish.

Grilled Pickerel

A hinged fish basket is a must for this dish. The White Wine Butter Sauce is excellent for serving over shellfish or as a basting sauce for grilled fish. You can prepare the sauce up to 3 days in advance, refrigerate, then warm in a small saucepan on the grill, stirring until it's just softened.

Pickerel

White Wine Butter Sauce:
1 cup unsalted butter, softened *236mL*
1/4 cup finely chopped shallots *59mL*

1/2 cup dry white wine *118mL*
2 tbsp finely chopped fresh parsley *30mL*
2 tsp lemon juice *10mL*
salt and pepper

Prepare the marinade: in a small heavy-bottomed saucepan melt 2 tbsp/30mL butter over medium-low heat. Add shallots and cover. Cook, stirring from time to time until very soft (about 8 minutes). Turn heat up to medium-high and add the wine, cooking for about 3 minutes or until wine is reduced to 1/3 cup/79mL. Remove from heat and whisk in the remaining butter. Stir in parsley and lemon juice. Season with salt and pepper to taste. Store in an airtight container.

Prepare fish basket by brushing with oil or spraying with non-stick cooking spray. To grill fish, lightly brush with White Wine Butter Sauce. Place in fish basket and grill over very hot coals, 10 minutes for each inch (2.5 cm) of fish at the thickest point. Brush with sauce from time to time. Fish will be opaque when cooked. Serve with ember-cooked vegetables and White Wine Butter Sauce on the side.

Parmesan Mackerel

Cheese lovers to forks for a feast of goodness.

4 lb mackerel, dressed (cleaned with head removed) *1.82kg*	1 tsp dry basil *5mL*
1/2 cup salad oil *118mL*	1 cup grated Parmesan cheese *236mL*
1/2 cup lemon juice *118mL*	1/2 tsp garlic salt *2.5mL*
2 tbsp chopped parsley *30mL*	

Rinse fish in cold water and wipe with a clean damp cloth. Combine oil, lemon juice, parsley and basil. Pour over fish and marinate for 1 hour. On wax paper, combine cheese and garlic salt. Coat fish in cheese mixture and place fish on grill. Cook, turning once, until fish flakes easily.

Bagged Fish

Paper bag cooking is fun, mostly because it is unexpected. Use a sturdy brown paper bag and lightly brush it with olive oil, on the inside.

Season your fish fillets or whole small fish, to taste. I like to brush them with butter and sprinkle with fresh tarragon. You could use rosemary or sage. If using whole fish place a little butter and herbs inside as well. Place in bag and fold the end over a few times and staple closed. Place on barbecue rack and judge cooking time by thickness of fish. If you are leary about the paper bag use foil.

Mushroom-Stuffed Whole Fish

Use this stuffing for whole baked Arctic char, lake whitefish, salmon, trout or any other firm-fleshed whole fish, or for any rolled fish fillets. This is enough for a large fish or 3-4 smaller ones.

1/4 cup butter *59mL*	3/4 cup crackers, coarsley crushed *177mL*
1/3 cup celery, chopped *79mL*	1/4 tsp poultry seasoning *1.25mL*
1/3 cup onion, minced *79mL*	
1 cup mushrooms, sliced *236mL*	1/4 tsp fennel or dried dill weed *1.25mL*
1 tbsp parsley, chopped *15mL*	

In a saucepan melt butter and sauté celery and onion 3-4 minutes, until golden brown. Add mushrooms and cook for 2 minutes more. Remove from heat. Stir in remaining ingredients and mix well.

Season the cavity of the fish with salt and pepper then press in stuffing. Sew cavity closed. Butter foil, lay fish on, butter top of fish then seal foil. Cook 10 minutes for each inch (2.5 cm) of thickness of the stuffed fish. You can also cook it in a wire fish basket basting frequently with a marinade or basting butter.

Cheesey Swiss Herring

The lady who gave me this recipe said it should be prepared with herring that have had the backbone removed. I admit I cannot do that, so I used herring fillets and tied them with wet string. If you use whole, deboned herring they cook up very well in a hinged wire fish basket.

4 herring fillets with skin left on or 2 deboned whole herring	pinch curry powder (optional)
salt and pepper	dash Worcester sauce
1 tbsp prepared mustard (French style) *15mL*	Swiss Gruyere cheese

Pat inside of fish dry with a paper towel then season lightly with salt and pepper. Mix mustard with Worcester sauce and curry. Spread inside of fish with this mixture then grill until lightly browned on each side. Remove fish, place slices of Gruyere inside, tie and return to grill until melted cheese oozes from fish. If using fillets, tie or carefully place in a hinged grill basket closed tightly so that cheese doesn't slip from between fillets, cook with skin side out. Serves 2

Indian River Stuffed Trout

When I make this I roughly chop about a cupful of celery, onion and some mushrooms, place them in an electric mini food chopper which finely chops, almost minces them. The rest of the mushrooms are left in larger slices. I find with the short cooking time needed this helps the flavor to blend in the stuffing.

1 large trout, cleaned
foil
butter
salt and pepper

Julie's stuffing:
1/8 cup celery *30mL*

1/4 cup mushrooms *59mL*
1/8 cup onion *30mL*
2 tbsp butter *30mL*
1/2 cup pine nuts *118mL*
2 slices bread, cut into small
  cubes

To prepare stuffing sauté celery, mushrooms, onion and pine nuts in sauté butter until lightly brown, add bread and toss until moistened. In the meantime, wash the trout (remove the head if desired or if fish is too long for barbecue), pat the inside dry then dust with salt and pepper. Brush foil, where trout will lie, with butter then place fish on foil and stuff.

Many cookbooks will tell you to close the fish with skewers or sew it closed. I don't; I find the foil holds it together well enough. It's your choice.

Butter the top of the fish then tightly secure the foil around it so that no steam can escape. Place over medium-hot coals and cook 10-15 minutes depending on thickness of fish. Turn and continue cooking until done. Check by unwrapping and gently test with a knife to see if fish flakes away from the bone. Keep wrapped until ready to eat. Delicious!

Crab Meat Wine Stuffing

This recipe came from the Culinary Institute of Canada located in Charlottetown, Prince Edward Island. We used it in haddock and it was delicious.

1 cup cooked crab meat *236mL*
2 ounces butter *60mL*
1/2 small onion, minced
1/2 tsp basil *2.5mL*
1/8 tsp rosemary *.63mL*
1/4 cup Rhine wine *59mL*

1/4 tsp salt *1.25mL*
1/8 tsp pepper *.63mL*
1 tbsp chopped parsley *15mL*
1 stalk celery, chopped
2 cups cracker crumbs *472mL*

Melt butter in saucepan over medium flame; add onion, basil, rosemary, salt, pepper and celery; sauté gently for 5 minutes, or until onion is golden brown. Celery need not be soft. Remove from heat.

Place cracker crumbs in large mixing bowl, add parsley and sauteed seasonings, blend well; add crab meat, mix thoroughly. Add enough Rhine wine to slightly moisten stuffing. For smaller fish use half of the amounts.

Shellfish

Oysters, clams, quahogs, cherrystone clams (small quahogs), scallops, mussels, crab, lobster, periwinkles—and other shellfish all barbecue nicely. Methods are generally determined by the size, structure and shape of each. All shellfish should be cleaned as close to cooking time as possible.

MUSSELS, CLAMS & OYSTERS IN THE SHELL

Nothing can be simpler than cooking shellfish over hot coals. Mussels, clams and oysters, in particular, come with their own cooking container and just have to be washed before popping on the grill. That makes them perfect for a shoreside or backyard barbecue. A grill set over hot coals in a fireplace ring works just great, as does a barbecue.

Just before you plan to cook shellfish, clean them by rubbing the shells with a brush and then rinsing off. The number of clams, mussels or oysters you serve depends on the people you are feeding. Those who live near the sea and have regular access to shellfish can consume copious quantities of them, especially if they have a nice dipping sauce or melted butter along side. If not frequent feasters, allow 6-8 per person.

Big bowls for shells are a necessary part of the table setting.

Cooking by laying directly on a grill over hot coals means that the mussel, clam or oyster cooks in its own juice. The steam caused by this liquid boiling in the shell forces it to open. If shell remains closed, discard. Excercise some care removing the shells from the grill as the liquid will scald if it is spilled on your skin. But ... don't tip it away, the juice is delicious.

CLAMS Cooking time depends on the size of the clams. Generally they take 5-7 minutes. They are done when they gape open. Discard any that open just slightly, or not at all.

MUSSELS Grill from 3 to 5 minutes or until the shell gapes open and the meat comes away from the shell. Discard any that do not open.

OYSTERS Place oysters on the grill with the flat side up, for 4-6 minutes or until slightly opened. Tip the juice into a bowl or discard. Hold the oyster in an oven mitt and insert a knife to twist off the flat shell. It may be necessary to cut the oyster from the flat shell. Serve in the rounded shell.

Serve with Lemon Garlic Butter (see p 87), Red Pepper and Tomato Dipping Sauce (see p 80), or another one of the dipping sauces or butters in this book.

STEAMING MUSSELS AND CLAMS ON THE BARBECUE

Laying mussels and clams on the grill works fine, but sometimes if we are in a hurry or don't want to bother with anything that fiddly, we just wrap up bundles of shellfish in aluminum foil. You don't need to add liquid, but can put in a splash of white wine or water, even beer, before sealing. Remember to seal the foil loosely to allow expansion room for opening shells and steam. Place bundles on the grill and remove as soon as shells have opened or steam is escaping from the package. Leave them wrapped and they will stay warm for a longer time. Serve with dipping sauces or butters.

Grilled Clams Parmesan

Serve with hot buttered French bread. Great finger food for a grill 'n' chat session (see p 15).

12 small fresh, hard-shell clams or oysters in the shell	1 tbsp lemon juice *15mL* 1/8 tsp garlic powder *.63mL*
3 tbsp butter or margarine, melted *45mL*	2 tsp grated Parmesan Cheese *10mL*

Scrub clams in cold water; drain in colander. Mix butter, lemon juice and garlic powder.

Arrange clams directly on grill 4-6 inches (10-15 cm) above hot coals and cook 2½ to 3 minutes. When partially open, remove the top shells. Drizzle clams with butter mixture, then sprinkle with parmesan. Continue to cook 2 to 3 minutes until cheese is golden.

Note: Our friends adore these clams but we find when feeding a crowd it gets too complicated to steam the clams open on the grill. They get eaten as soon as they open. We usually have a big crowd in so I steam clams in a pot and plunk it on the table. The lemon/garlic/butter mixture is there, as is the Parmesan. Some can't wait, they just dig in to the clams and go for the Parmesan Grill once their voracious appetites are sated. Others go for them right from the beginning and practically hang over the grill, guarding their treasure as their mouths water and nostrils twitch.

They are great appetizers and can be broiled in a single layer, 4-5 inches/10-15cm from the heat source.

Hint: If I have lots of garlic on hand I mince it instead of using the powder. We use this butter mixture for dunking any shellfish.

Simple Scallops in Bacon

Scallops are wonderful for grilling because of the simplicity of preparation and cooking. They are most often cooked on skewers so check out the shish kebab section. This recipe is simplicity in itself and great for parties because it can be prepared ahead and cooks up quickly as needed.

scallops	toothpicks
bacon slices, cut into half	

Wrap each scallop in bacon and secure with a toothpick. Cook on a medium hot grill. When the bacon is cooked, so is the scallop.

Elegant Scallops in Bacon

I use this recipe when I have those great big evenly-sized scallops and I want to make a special effort for company.

1 lb scallops *454g*	1/8 tsp pepper *.63mL*
1/4 cup salad oil *59mL*	1/4 lb sliced bacon *113g*
2 tbsp lemon juice *30mL*	paprika
1 tsp salt *5mL*	

Drain scallops. Place in a bowl. Combine oil, lemon juice, salt and pepper. Pour this mixture over the scallops and let stand for up to 30 minutes, stirring from time to time. Cut each piece of bacon in half lengthwise, then crosswise. Fry bacon until just cooked but not crisp. Remove scallops; reserve sauce for basting. Wrap each scallop with a piece of bacon and fasten with a wooden toothpick. Place in an oiled hinged wire grill basket and cook over hot coals for about 5 minutes, then baste, sprinkle with paprika, turn and cook for a further 5-7 minutes until bacon is crisp and scallop cooked.

Scallops Oriental

You need a hinged grill basket for these sweet, succulent scallops. Serve with other oriental dishes and rice for a theme meal.

2 pounds scallops *908 g*	1/4 cup prepared mustard *59mL*
Oriental Basting Sauce:	2 tsp curry powder *10mL*
1/4 cup honey *59mL*	1 tsp lemon juice *5mL*

Mix sauce ingredients well. Place scallops closely together in a rectangular hinged grill basket which has been sprayed with non-stick cooking spray. Brush scallops generously on both sides with basting sauce. Grill over low heat for 10-20 minutes depending on the size of the scallops, turning and basting often. They will brown nicely.

Crisp Newfie Scallops

This recipe, which came to me from Newfoundland is great for those people who think seafood has to be breaded to be good. This eliminates the fat of deep frying. Serve with Tartar Sauce (see index).

1 lb scallops, thaw if frozen, rinse and drain well *454g*	1/8 tsp pepper *.63mL*
1/4 tsp salt *1.25mL*	1/3 cup melted butter *79mL*
	1/2 cup fine breadcrumbs *118mL*

Season scallops with salt and pepper; dip them in butter then roll in crumbs. Place in an oiled, hinged wire grill basket and grill 8-10 minutes, turning to brown evenly. Serves 4

King Crab Legs

Crab legs can be cooked right on the grill over a low heat. It takes about 15 minutes. Don't turn them over, or they will lose their juices and dry out.

Serve with a dipping sauce such as English Pub Seafood Sauce (p 81) or Lemon Chive Sauce (76); along with lobster crackers and picks, or scissors to open legs.

Italian King Crab Legs

If frozen, thaw legs. Split lengthwise using scissors and lift off the smaller half of the shell. Baste with Italian dressing. Cook over medium heat, flesh-side up for 10 minutes. Turn and grill a few more minutes until done.

I really like using an Italian dressing that has Parmesan cheese in it.

Lemon Garlic Crab Legs

Prepare crab legs as above substituting Lemon Garlic Butter (see p 87) for Italian Dressing.

Grilled Prawns

Prawns, or jumbo shrimp, are a North American favorite in everything from salads to pizzas. Just wait till the population discovers how good they can be when prepared on the grill. After shelling and deveining them try some of the following:

Large prawns and garlic butter (about 2 tbsp/30 mL for six large prawns) can be wrapped in foil and grilled for 10-12 minutes.

or

Butterfly (cut almost in half starting at front so that they spread out like butterfly wings) large prawns; marinate for 10-15 minutes then place on grill over low coals for about 5 minutes, turning once and basting often. They are done when they become pink and firm — be careful not to overcook. Simply excellent served with avocado and London Seafood Sauce (see p 81) or Tropical Dip (see p 80).

Shrimp Creole

This recipe from the New Brunswick Department of Fisheries has travelled back up the long journey that the Acadians travelled in 1760 after they were expelled from the Maritimes. Creole and Cajun, derivation of Acadian, cuisine live cheek by jowl in Louisiana — the one from southern origins, the latter from the north.

8 oz jumbo shrimp *227g*
1 tbsp cornstarch *15mL*
2 tbsp butter *30mL*
2 cups cooked rice *472mL*
1 1/2 cups chopped mushrooms *354mL*
2 tbsp chopped onion *30mL*
1/4 cup chopped green pepper *59mL*

1 can (14 oz or *420mL*) supreme tomatoes
1/4 cup chili sauce *59mL*
1/2 tsp oregano *2.5mL*
1/2 tsp basil *2.5mL*
1/2 tsp parsley *2.5mL*
1-2 cloves garlic, minced
1/4 tsp thyme *1.25mL*
salt and pepper to taste

Peel and devein shrimp. Roll in cornstarch. Butter one large piece of heavy-duty foil. Place shrimp on foil; cover with rice, mushrooms, onion and green pepper. Chop tomatoes and mix well with seasonings. Pour over vegetables. Seal foil with double folds. Cook about 10 minutes or until flesh is opaque. Serves 2-3

Grilled Lobster

Most people never consider cooking lobster on the barbecue, at least where we live, because the traditional method is to steam them. However, that should change. The crustacean is wonderful grilled. The experts say the best method is to cut a live lobster in half, remove the brain area and grill it using an herbed butter. Start the cut at the head.

lobster, split and cleaned   garlic or herb basting butter
or lobster tails, split

Brush lobster with a little butter on both sides. Lay on grill, shell down for about 3 minutes then brush with butter again and turn, cooking for another 2-4 minutes. Serve with the herb butter or a dipping sauce.

Spiny or Rock Lobster Tails

Can be cooked as above but should be split down the centre as the shell is tough and can be difficult to cut when cooked. Keep basting them with butter to prevent drying and toughening of the meat. Watch carefully and serve as soon as they are cooked.

Periwinkles

These little snails are prolific at the seashore and, in the right location, can be picked by the bucket full, which is good because you need 18 to 24 per person. Periwinkles must be boiled or steamed just until the hard shell or lid falls open. Then take a straight pin or needle and ease the spiral shapped meat from the shell. Discard the lid and eat the winkles with melted butter (herb or garlic butter is a nice accompaniment for this meat which has a slight nutty flavor).

To cook on the barbecue wrap periwinkles in foil bundles and steam or place in a shallow pan of boiling water or wine. Melt butter in another small saucepan.

This is a fun addition to a picnic at the shore. Send the kids off with pails to gather dinner. Once the adults have eaten the meat from the periwinkles, the children will have clean shells to take home.

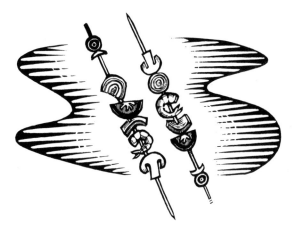

Shish Kebabs
or
Skewer Cooking

T he skewer, or cooking stick was in all likelihood the first cooking utensil. In culinary lore it is suggested that shortly after primitive man amazed himself by discovering how to build and control a fire, he somehow tuned in to the idea that food tasted better and was more palatable when cooked.

Can't you picture a cave-man type, mouthwatering at the delicious smokey aroma of cooking meat or fish, burning his fingers as he tried to extract it from a fire. The first utensil used to remove food from the embers was a skewer, a stick or a piece of bone, and at the same time it was obvious that pieces of meat could be cooked on the skewer, either held over the heat or left on the skewer.

Since those early beginnings charbroiling over an open fire has become part of the genetic makeup of all peoples. Every major cuisine in the world uses skewers to cook. The shish kebabs of Greece, brochettes of France, satays of Indonesia, the fish and hare of the North American Indian, even the marshmallow that has become part of our culture all need a skewer of sorts.

Today you can get finely honed, cast and decorative metal spears that are a beautiful part of table decor. Most of us use simple metal skewers. There are some great long ones on the market for use when camping.

For home barbecuing I prefer bamboo skewers which come from the Orient. They are short enough to fit well on the hibachi or portable gas barbecues; they don't get hot enough to burn your fingers and are cheap and disposable. Another plus is that they are thinner, thus better to use with seafood.

You might find on occasion that the flat metal skewers are better for fish because they won't "roll" within the fish, thus causing it to slip around.

Kebabs on skewers are wonderful when the cook is in a hurry to satisfy ravenous guests. Because the food must be cut into small pieces, they are easily prepared and cook quickly. More of the cooking surface is exposed, giving a wonderful charbroiled flavor. You can determine how foods cook by how you put them on the skewer. If strung loosely it will be well done in the same time a tightly strung kabob is cooked rare to medium. Food strung tightly together will stay moister.

Another big plus for kebabs is that food can be stretched to feed more with less by combining with fruits and vegetables.

Fancy garnishes, sauces or plate presentation are usually not a concern with kebabs. If an attractive presentation is desired for a party or special cookout, then the precutting of colorful ingredients shapes the finished dish and a marinade, or basting sauce can add a simple, yet savory flavor.

You need a sturdy fish, such as tuna (fresh), swordfish, halibut or salmon. Shellfish, such as shrimp and scallops, are perfect.

Fruit, pineapple, apple, lemon—anything that will stay on a skewer—can be interspersed with seafood. Just about any vegetable will be good. The trick is to choose those with similar cooking times to the seafood such as mushrooms, tomato, onion. Longer cooking items can be started ahead on separate skewers. If you are not basting, brush vegetables lightly with olive oil to prevent them from drying out.

Don't hesitate to add interest to kebabs by using your imagination. Cocktail weiners, pieces of sausage (prick well and precook until just pink in the middle, then cut into 1-inch/2.5cm pieces) or even chunks of salami or pepperoni make interesting additions to seafood kebabs, especially if using a tomato based basting sauce.

Grilled Lemon Shrimp

When we cook these I eat them lemon and all. The olive oil and fresh basil make for delightful nibbling. Just be careful not to overcook.

16 uncooked large shrimps or prawns (if they are on the small side increase number to 24)

Marinade:
1 cup dry white wine *236mL*

1 cup olive oil *236mL*
1/2 cup chopped fresh basil or lemon verbena *118mL*
1 tbsp coarsely cracked black pepper *15mL*

8 bamboo skewers, soaked for 1 hour in water
8 thin lemon slices

Combine marinade ingredients. Peel and devein shrimp, leaving tail on. Place shrimp in bowl and cover with marinade. Cover and refrigerate at least 3 hours, turning occasionally.

Heat the barbecue to a high heat. Drain shrimp, reserving marinade. Thread skewer through tail and head of shrimp, then a piece of lemon twisted into an "S" shape, a shrimp and more lemon; divide them evenly between the 8 skewers. Grill shrimp until just opaque, basting occasionally with reserved marinade, about 3 minutes per side. Sprinkle with fresh basil to serve.

Grilled Shrimp

We were told to put shrimp into an oiled grilling basket or set on an oiled wire cake rack on the grill so that the shrimp wouldn't fall through. Since we didn't have one, we put them on skewers and they were fine.

30 jumbo shrimp
12 bamboo skewers, soaked in water for at least one hour

Shrimp Marinade:
1½ tsp finely chopped garlic *7.5mL*
2 small shallots (or mild onion), chopped fine to make about 2 tbsp/*30mL*
1/4 cup tarragon vinegar *59mL*

1½ tbsp Dijon mustard *22.5mL*
1 tsp salt *5mL*
1/2 tsp freshly ground pepper *2.5mL*
1/4 tsp dried tarragon leaves *1.25mL*
2/3 cup vegetable oil *157mL*
1/3 cup olive oil *79mL*
3 tbsp chopped fresh parsley *45mL*

Place garlic, shallots, vinegar, mustard, salt, pepper and tarragon in a blender or food processor and mix well. Continue to blend slowly while adding oils through opening in cover in a slow steady stream. Blend until thick and creamy. Pour into a large bowl and stir in parsley, then add shrimp turning to coat well. Cover and refrigerate at least 6 hours, preferably overnight.

When ready to grill, drain shrimp reserving marinade for basting. Put in oiled grill basket or thread on bamboo skewers. Cook 4-6 inches/10-15cm above hot coals 1½ to 2 minutes per side, basting once until shrimp are pink and barely opaque in the center. Makes 6 main dish or 10 appetizer servings.

Scallop/Prawn Surprise

This dish is ideal for company. It's one my mom came up with, a gourmet delight offering two distinctive flavours. We like it served with a Caesar salad, fresh Italian bread slathered in butter, and Pineapple/Honey kebabs (see p 75) for dessert. The beauty of entertaining with this meal is that everything can be prepared ahead. If you wish to do that put scallops and prawns on separate skewers and marinate them in long narrow dishes, right on the skewer otherwise prepare as below.

1 lb scallops of uniform size
   454g

Scallop Marinade:
1/2 cup pineapple juice *118mL*
1/2 cup sherry *118mL*
1 lb prawns of uniform size *454g*

Prawn Marinade:
3/4 cup sherry *177mL*
1/4 cup soya sauce *59mL*
1 tsp sugar (optional) *5mL*
1/2 tsp ground ginger *2.5mL*
whole mushrooms
melted butter
sesame seeds

Prepare scallops by rinsing and patting dry with paper towels. Mix pineapple juice and sherry and marinate the scallops in this mixture for at least an hour.

Shell and wash prawns, removing black line over back, pat dry with paper towels. Combine sherry, soya sauce, sugar and ginger and marinate prawns in this mixture at least an hour.

Drain both, then thread two scallops on one end of skewer, a mushroom, then two prawns (bend so that the skewer goes through each prawn twice).

Brush each kebab with melted butter then roll in the sesame seeds.

Cook over medium heat for 5 minutes, turn carefully. If they seem to be drying at all, drizzle the remaining marinade carefully over them being careful not to wash off the seeds. Be sure to use the correct marinade on each one. Cook for a further 4-5 minutes if large shellfish are used. Don't overcook.

The number this will serve depends on how large the shellfish are and how many you serve. We usually plan 2 kebabs per person.

Scallops en Brochette

Skewer whole scallops, medium-sized mushrooms and squares of bacon. Grill over charcoal about 10 minutes, turning often and brushing with a highly seasoned French dressing throughout the cooking.

NORTHERN SHARK The northern shark is a relatively new fish in the North American marketplace even though it has been in high demand in Europe for years. The British especially value it for those legendary fish and chips. Found on both coasts of the North American continent, it is fished from southern Labrador down to North Carolina. One of the reasons for its popularity is the bone-free meat and for barbecuers the fact that the firm, medium-fat flesh will not fall apart in cooking. The white fleshed shark has some dark meat that is unique in its flavor—sweet and delicate.

The experts at the Nova Scotia Department of Fisheries tell me that shark often has a slight ammonia odor. This is natural in fish that has been properly handled and is caused by a natural chemical occurrence. This odor dissipates during cooking; however, to remove the odor completely, you can marinate shark in an acidic solution such as lemon juice or a vinegar/water solution.

A medium-fat fish, best cooked over the barbecue, it needs to be basted as it does not contain enough fat and is not self-basting. A combination of seasoned oil and vinegar is excellent for basting or use one of the marinades listed in this book. Recipes for northern shark should have an acidic base, such as lemon, orange or pineapple juice. Those using tomatoes are also excellent.

Brightly Skewered Northern Shark

1 lb northern shark fillets *454g*
2 small zucchini, 1 inch/*2.5cm*
    cubes
1 red pepper, 1 inch/*2.5cm*
    cubes

1 green pepper, 1 inch/*2.5cm*
    cubes

Shark Marinade:
1/4 cup olive oil *59mL*
1/4 cup lemon juice *59mL*
1/2 tsp tarragon *2.5mL*

Pat dry fillets and cut in 1-inch/2.5cm cubes. Combine olive oil, lemon juice and tarragon; mix well. Add fish and stir to coat all fish pieces with marinade. Refrigerate 1 hour.

Toss vegetables in with fish to coat in marinade. Remove with slotted spoon, reserving marinade to use for basting. Place fish and vegetables alternately on skewers. Barbecue or broil 4 inches/10cm from heat source for about 10 minutes, turning fish to brown all sides. Baste skewers with drained marinade while cooking. Serves 4

Nova Scotia Northern Shark Kebabs

1 lb northern shark fillets, 1
    inch/*2.5cm cubes 454g*
16 mushrooms
16 cherry tomatoes

Kebabs Marinade:
1/2 cup lemon juice *118mL*

1/2 cup vegetable oil *118mL*
2 tbsp minced parsley *30mL*
1 tsp dry mustard *5mL*
1 med clove garlic, minced
salt to taste (optional)
1/4 tsp pepper *1.25mL*

Stir marinade mixture until blended in a large bowl. Add fish to marinade, stirring so that all is covered. Refrigerate 45 minutes. Just before assembling kebabs, stir in mushrooms and tomato. Then thread on skewers alternating mushroom, tomato and fish. Reserve remaining marinade to use to baste during cooking. Grill 4 inches/10cm from heat, for about 10 minutes, turning to brown on all sides. Serves 4

Fish and Fruit Kebabs

Another "southern style" recipe adapted by New Brunswick Fisheries.

8 oz jumbo shrimp, shelled and deveined *227g*
8 oz fish cubes (shark, monkfish, halibut, cusk, catfish and salmon work well — so do scallops) *227g*
2 oranges, in sections
2 nectarines or peaches, in sections or chunks
green grapes

Orange Soy Marinade:
1/3 cup orange juice *79mL*
1/4 cup vegetable oil *59mL*
2 tbsp soya sauce *30mL*
1 tbsp grated orange rind *15mL*
1 tsp ground ginger *5mL*
1/2 tsp salt *2.5mL*
1/2 tsp pepper *2.5mL*

Mix marinade ingredients, blending well. Pour over seafood and fruits and marinate for 30 minutes at room temperature or 1 hour in refrigerator, mixing well once or twice. Thread on oiled skewers, alternating seafood and fruits. Grill 5 minutes on one side, baste, turn and grill another 4 to 6 minutes or until flesh is opaque. Baste often. Serves 4

Honey Barbecued Kebabs

8 oz scallops *227g*
8 oz fish fillets, see above suggestions *227g*
1 green pepper, cubed
1 onion, cut in wedges
12 mushrooms

Honey Barbecue Marinade:
1/4 cup lemon juice *59mL*
3 tbsp vegetable oil *45mL*
2 tbsp honey *30mL*
1 tbsp soya sauce *15mL*
1 tbsp oyster sauce *15mL*
1/2 tsp ground nutmeg *2.5mL*

Mix marinade ingredients, pour over fish and vegetables and marinate 30 minutes, stirring from time to time. Thread on oiled skewers. Grill 5 minutes and turn to grill another 4-6 minutes, basting often. Serves 4

Summer Cooler Kebabs

2 lb seafood (monkfish, catfish, cusk, shark, swordfish, scallops or any combination) *908g*
30 cantaloupe balls
30 honeydew melon balls
1/4 cup lemon juice *59mL*

2 tbsp melted butter *30mL*
1/4 cup Brie cheese (cut into chunks) *59mL*
1/4 cup blend (light cream) *59mL*
wild rice, prepared ready to eat with kebabs

Alternate seafood, cantaloupe and melon on 6 skewers, beginning and ending with seafood. Mix lemon juice and melted butter in a small dish. Brush over kebabs and grill about 10 minutes, turning to brown evenly. Baste frequently. In a small saucepan on the back of the grill melt Brie cheese and gradually whisk in blend until smooth. Drizzle cheese mixture over kebabs and continue cooking until golden brown. Serve on a bed of wild rice with a deep green salad, for a prize-winning meal.

Note: This can be a bit messy, especially on a gas barbecue, so lay a foil drip-catcher over your coals to prevent smoking. If using scallops alone, cut amount to 1-1½ pounds/454-681g.

Salmon Teriyaki on Skewers

This cooks up fast and is lovely served as part of an oriental theme meal. We like it with rice, snow peas steamed in foil, and skewered mushrooms. If serving with steamed rice lay the salmon on the rice and drizzle a little of the sauce over to serve.

2 pounds salmon steak or thick fillets, cut in 1 or 2-inch/2.5-5cm chunks *908kg*

Teriyaki Sauce:
1/3 cup soy sauce *79mL*
1/3 cup rice wine or dry sherry *79mL*

1/2 clove garlic, minced
1/2 tsp finely chopped fresh ginger root *2.5mL*
1 green onion, finely chopped
bamboo skewers, soaked in water for 10 minutes

Pat salmon pieces dry then thread on skewers and place on a hot grill, turning at least once. While cooking mix together the sauce ingredients and boil 1 minute. After salmon has cooked for 3 minutes, brush with sauce, turn and continue cooking, turning and basting until salmon is cooked. Total time should be no longer than 7-8 minutes, depending on size of chunks.

In Tandem

Beef Wrapped Oysters

I first had this at a friends home and had an awful job getting the recipe. However two bottles of wine and one large headache later I wrote it on the back of my chequebook. It was worth the effort. This stuffing also works well in whole fish.

2 large slices of beef cut very thin (or you could buy a thick steak and slit it like an envelope)

Oyster Stuffing:
1 cup fresh oysters, shucked 236 mL
or 1 — 5 oz/ not smoked 1-150 mL can
4 tbsp fresh bread crumbs 60 mL
1 tbsp melted butter *15 mL*
1 tbsp finely chopped onion *15 mL*
1 tbsp finely chopped chives (if no fresh chives are available double the onion) *15 mL*
1 tbsp finely chopped parsley (optional) *15 mL*
1 tbsp pine nuts *15 mL*
1-2 tbsp lemon juice *15-30 mL*
pepper to taste

Mix all stuffing ingredients. Divide stuffing and lay on the steak then fold the meat closed as you would an envelope. Sew or tie so that the meat will not spill the stuffing. Barbecue over medium-high coals, turning only once. If the oysters are fresh, they will require a little more cooking than canned ones—medium steak should give a hot stuffing. Cooking time depends on the thickness of the steak.

Note: If desired, use a hot tomato barbecue sauce on the outside of the steak.

Crab-Stuffed Chicken

8 whole chicken breasts, boned
1 egg, well beaten
1 cup packaged herb-seasoned
   stuffing *236 mL*
1-10 oz can Campbell's
   condensed cream of shrimp
   soup, divided *1-300 mL can*
1-7 oz can crab meat, drained
   and flaked *1-198g can*
1/4 cup chopped green pepper
   59 mL

1 tbsp lemon juice *15 mL*
2 tsp Worcestershire sauce
   10 mL
1 tsp prepared mustard *5 mL*
1/4 tsp salt *1.25 mL*
1/4 tsp cooking oil *1.25 mL*
1 tsp teriyaki sauce
1/4 tsp onion juice *1.25 mL*
dash pepper

Combine egg, stuffing, 1/2 cup/118 mL soup, crab meat, green pepper, lemon juice, Worcestershire sauce, mustard and salt. Mix well. Place dressing on chicken breasts, fold meat around mixture and close with skewers. If you have trouble keeping these closed use a grill basket for cooking so that they won't unroll.

Grill over medium hot coals, for 30 minutes, or until tender, turning frequently.

Combine remaining soup with oil, teriyaki sauce, onion juice, and pepper, and heat through. Top each serving with sauce.

Gourmet Shrimp Stuffed Porterhouse

4 porterhouse (or rib-eye, strip
   loin or tenderloin) steaks each
   1¼ inches/*3 cm thick*

Shrimp Stuffing:
2 tbsp butter *30 mL*
1/4 cup finely chopped onion
   59 mL
1/2 cup finely chopped celery
   118 mL
1 cup canned baby shrimp
   236 mL

1/4 cup fine bread crumbs
   59 mL
1 tbsp lemon juice *15 mL*
1 tbsp dry white wine *15 mL*
salt, pepper, parsley and savory
   to taste

Steak Basting Sauce:
1/4 cup dry red wine *59 mL*
2 tbsp soy sauce *30 mL*

Sauté onions and celery in butter until tender-crisp; then add the remaining stuffing ingredients, heating through. Cut a deep pocket in the side of each steak. Fill pocket with stuffing mixture and skewer closed. Barbecue steak over medium-hot coals for approximately 20 minutes or until desired doneness, turning once and brushing with steak basting sauce. Serves 4-8

Nibblers
&
Finger Foods

Picture a yard party on a hot summer's eve—a gathering where friends chit chat their way around the lawn and cold drinks and finger foods are the order of the day. There you have the place where the barbecue can really prove a hit, especially if loaded with nibblers.

Nothing should need a knife, a fork or a plate—just fingers, so it should either be cooked on small skewers or toothpicks. Any kebab recipe will work, just cut bamboo skewers in half so they hold 2-3 pieces. Try these favorites from our house.

Porkers Nibbles

Hickory-flavored bacon is delicious with seafood!

Shark chunks about 1 inch/ *2.5cm square* (mako, blue, or northern shark work well, as do other firm, fatty fish such as monkfish, swordfish, catfish, cusk and mackerel) or prawns, scallops and chunks of crabmeat or any combination of the above bacon slices, halved

Wrap bite-sized pieces of seafood in bacon, secure with a wooden toothpick and grill over hot coals until bacon is crisp. Serve with a dipping sauce, hot English mustard or as they are.

Mussel Stuffed Mushrooms

These can be baked at 450 F/232C in the oven or cooked on the grill with the lid down. Delicious.

32 large fresh mushrooms
32 mussels, steamed and
   removed from shells
1 cup unsalted butter, softened
   236mL
2 tsp garlic, minced *10mL*
2 tbsp green onion, chopped
   very fine *30mL*

2 tbsp parsley, chopped fine
   30mL
1/2 tsp salt *2.5mL*
1/4 tsp pepper *1.25mL*
1/2 cup packaged breadcrumbs
   118mL
1 lemon cut into eighths

In a small bowl, blend 3/4 cup/177mL butter with garlic, onion, parsley, salt and pepper. Melt the remaining butter in a large skillet. Add breadcrumbs and toss in butter to coat. Remove from heat.

Remove stems from mushrooms. Arrange caps, bottom up on a tray. If desired you can brush bottom of each with butter, but it isn't necessary. Place mussel in each cap, top with 1 tsp/5mL butter and breadcrumbs. Cover and refrigerate until ready to cook. Place on medium grill and cook until butter is melted and mushroom is cooked, 5-10 minutes depending on size.

Vegetables
& Fruit
on the Grill

If the coals are hot why not cook vegetables on the grill along with seafood. They look wonderful as well as being nutritious and tasty. Several tips for cooking vegetables appear throughout this book so check the index.

Quick cooking vegetables can be grilled without any preliminary blanching. Just lightly brush them (except corn) with oil or your favorite oil-based salad dressing and grill along with other foods until slightly charred and crisp-tender. Almost any basting sauce or marinade for seafood can also be used on vegetables. If you are cooking for two this is an excellent way to utilize marinade when the recipe makes more than you need for seafood.

Here are a few additional tips:

GREEN ONIONS In a long shallow dish, marinate 12 large green onions in a mixture of 3/4 cup/177mL bottled Italian dressing and 2 tbsp/30mL each soy sauce and lemon juice for 15-20 minutes. Remove onions and reserve marinade for basting. Grill 5 inches/ 12.5cm above medium-hot coals 10-12 minutes, turning and basting 4 times until tender and slightly charred.

BELL AND FRYING PEPPERS Halve lengthwise, remove seeds and grill or broil about 10 minutes, turning and basting at least once.

PEPPERS—ROASTED Peppers used in sauces such as salsa are best skinned, deveined and seeded. You can use the barbecue to prepare peppers in this way.
Place peppers about 6 inches/15cm from heat source, turning frequently until they are black all over—about 10 minutes. Place peppers in a brown paper bag and leave 10 minutes. Peel, cut open and remove seeds and ribs. Chop finely and pat dry; you should have about 3/4 cup/177mL. Roasted peppers can be cut into strips and served with grilled fish. For extra color combine red, yellow and green peppers.

CORN Leave in the husk (no need to remove silks although I do) and soak in water for 10-15 minutes. Grill for 15-20 minutes, turning 3 or 4 times, until the husks are charred and the kernels are tender when pierced. Wear gloves or use a napkin or towel when you peel off the hot husks and silks.
Corn can also be cut into 1-2 inch/2.5-5cm pieces, parboiled then cooked on skewers. It's delicious when basted with one of our marinades or basting butters.

EGGPLANT AND SUMMER SQUASH Slice large ones into 1/2-inch/ 1.25 cm thick rounds. Cut small ones lengthwise into 1/4 inch/50 mm thick slices to about 1-inch/2.5cm thick from stem end. Fan out slices. Grill, basting and turning once, about 5 minutes per side for rounds, 7 minutes per side for fanned-out slices.
Slices of eggplant, 3/4 inch/1.88cm thick dredged lightly with flour, dotted with butter and brushed with oil are delicious broiled, as you would a burger. Turn once during cooking, brushing top lightly with oil, season with pepper and sprinkle with grated cheese.

MUSHROOMS Wipe with a damp cloth; thread on skewers. Grill 5 to 7 minutes depending on size, basting and turning twice. If you don't have a basting sauce at hand, use butter.

TOMATOES Cut large firm ripe tomatoes in half and cook cut sides down, basting and turning once until lightly browned and just tender. Skewer cherry tomatoes, baste and turn just until split. Take care not to overcook.

POTATOES Roast them by scraping a hollow in the coals, placing pototoes in hollow and raking the coals back over them Use large potatoes and roast 45-60 minutes
Cubes of potato can be parboiled then strung on kebabs. Baste during cooking. Round white varieties of potatoes are best for cooking on kebabs. Use bakers if cooking whole.

ZUCCHINI Cut thick slices and thread on kebabs to cook, basting while cooking.

ROOT VEGETABLES Carrots, turnip, and other root vegetables can be cut in pieces and used on kebabs or grilled directly on the grill as long as they have been parboiled. Baste with a seasoned butter.

Sherried Mushrooms

These are best prepared when you don't have a large crew to feed as they take up a lot of space on the grill.

1 lb large fresh mushrooms, brushed clean *454g*	1/4 cup sherry *59mL*
1/4 cup butter *59mL*	lemon pepper

Separate stems from mushroom caps and chop fine. Melt butter. Mix in sherry and chopped stems. Divide this mixture between the caps, sprinkle each with lemon pepper then place bottom up on the grill over a medium heat. Cooking time depends on size of mushrooms.

Note: If you have small mushrooms, place in foil bowl, drizzle with butter and/or sherry, sprinkle with lemon pepper and cook for 15-20 minutes over medium heat.

Herbed New Potatoes

Since we live in the province of "Bud The Spud" it is natural to bring you a recipe from the P.E.I. Dept of Agriculture. Garden herbs and new potatoes are ready together and superb together on the barbecue.

new potatoes sufficient for your crew	garlic clove, finely minced or garlic powder, to taste
butter	fresh basil, savory, thyme or dill weed

Cook potatoes in small amount of boiling, salted water for 10 minutes or until half-cooked. Drain and cool. Place each potato on a double layer of foil. Dot with butter and dash of garlic. Sprinkle with chopped fresh herbs of your choice. Wrap well and place on grill about 4 inches/10cm from medium hot coals; cook, turning occasionally, until tender, about 15 minutes.

Note: "New Potatoes" are those dug early from green tops; their immature skin "feathers" or rubs off in places. Other potatoes or mature potatoes have a set skin and have been dug much later in the season.

Stuffed Potatoes

Take a hint from those fast food outlets that have turned to the stuffed potato and cook up your own on the barbecue. Each stuffing below will do 4-6 baking potatoes.

large baking potatoes

Salmon stuffing: *Spinach Cheese stuffing:*

	or
Salmon stuffing:	*Spinach Cheese stuffing:*
7 oz can red salmon, drained *198g can*	1 cup spinach, cooked and drained *236mL*
1 tbsp sour cream *15mL*	1/2 cup grated cheddar or parmesan cheese *118mL*
2 green onions, finely chopped	2 shallots, chopped
1 gherkin or 1/2 dill pickle, finely chopped (optional)	1/4 tsp nutmeg *1.25mL*

Wrap potatoes in oiled foil, pierce top with fork and cook on grill with hood down, until tender. Cool slightly, cut off tops and scoop out inside of each potato, leaving 1/4 inch/.64 cm around the shell. Mash reserved potatoes and combine with stuffing ingredients and spoon back into potato skins. Rewrap with foil and return to the grill to heat through.

Adding fruit to your barbecue menu gives a wonderful South Seas flavor to the meal. Do experiment, it can be great fun and very rewarding for the taste buds.

Pineapple/Honey Kabobs

1 can pineapple pieces about 1 inch in size honey	butter cinnamon

Combine honey, butter and cinnamon. Put pineapple pieces on skewers. This looks nice if you buy slices and cut them into wedges then arrange in patterns. Grill over medium heat for about 15 minutes, basting often with honey-butter.

Rum-Soaked Oranges

4 oranges, peeled and white inner skin taken off, cut through almost to bottom (so that they are held together at bottom)	4 bananas, peeled and split rum brown sugar foil

Place each fruit on foil, sprinkle with rum and brown sugar then seal foil tightly. Grill 12-15 minutes on barbecue, depending on size of orange.

Coconut Peaches

4 large firm peaches, halved with stone removed 1/4 cup butter *59mL*	1/4 cup brown sugar *59mL* 1 cup shredded coconut *250mL* orange juice

Divide butter, brown sugar and coconut between 4 peaches. Place each on individual squares of foil, squeeze a little orange juice over each then seal in the foil. Grill about 15 minutes on the barbecue.

Kebabs

Fruit such as firm fresh strawberries, bananas, kiwis, cantaloupe and fresh pineapple can be used alone, together, or interspersed with seafood on kebabs. Baste while cooking, using one of the seafood marinades or a Rum Orange Basting Sauce (see p 86).

Sauces, Dips & Butters

Hot sauces are ideal for seafood as it cools down quickly after cooking. We have a very small saucepan for hot sauces which we keep on the back of the grill for 2 to 4 people. For a large crowd, use a fondue pot.

Lemon/Chive Hot Sauce

1/2 cup butter *118mL*
1/4 cup lemon juice *59mL*
1/4 cup white wine *59mL*

1 tbsp chives, chopped (or use your favourite herb) *15mL*

Melt butter, add rest of ingredients and keep warm until spooned over fish.

Maritime Lemon Butter

Keep this butter hot and use to dip lobster, clams, mussels and so on. If you are feeding a crowd increase proportionately and put in a fondue pot, providing a dipper and small bowls to be used individually. This is how Maritimers love shellfish : from shell to dip to mouth.

1/2 cup butter *118mL*	1 garlic clove minced or garlic
1/2 lemon	powder to taste

Put butter in a small pan or heat proof bowl by placing on the back of the grill. Squeeze the juice of the lemon into the butter and add garlic to taste.

Citrus Sauce

Add zing to your seafood

1 cup chicken bouillon *236mL*	1 tbsp lemon juice *15mL*
1 tsp cornstarch *5mL*	orange segments, if fresh, ease
2 tbsp orange rind *30mL*	out pips with a sharp knife
1/2 tsp orange juice *2.5mL*	

In a small saucepan heat chicken bouillon. Mix cornstarch with orange juice and blend into bouillon. Add remaining ingredients and stir until sauce thickens. Serve with orange segments.

Tangy Lemon Butter Sauce

1/4 cup melted butter *59mL*	1/4 tsp Tabasco pepper sauce
4 tsp lime or lemon juice *20mL*	*1.25mL*

Combine all ingredients. Use for basting or in individual serving cups for dipping seafood.

Oceanburger Sauce

This is great for kids and adults. For kids—or kids at heart—cook breaded fish on the grill by basting with butter, then serve on a bun with a spoonful of sauce and a slice of tomato. This sauce cooks up well on the back of the grill as it only needs to simmer.

1 — 11 oz can condensed
   Cheddar cheese soup,
   undiluted *330mL — can*
2 tsp lemon juice *10mL*
1 tsp Worcestershire sauce *5mL*

1/2 tsp onion flakes *2.5mL*
1/4 tsp Tabasco pepper sauce
   1.25mL
1/4 tsp crushed oregano *1.25mL*

Place all ingredients in a saucepan. Mix well. Simmer for 15 minutes, stirring from time to time. Spoon over grilled fish.

Horseradish Sauce

Toasted almonds give a distinctive touch to a zippy sauce.

1/4 cup sliced almonds *59mL*
2 tbsp butter *30mL*
2 tbsp all purpose flour *30mL*
1/4 tsp salt *1.25mL*

1 small can (*2/3 cup*) evaporated
   milk
1/3 cup milk *79mL*
2 tbsp prepared horseradish
   30mL

Sauté almonds in butter until golden brown using a small saucepan. Remove almonds and set aside. Stir in flour and salt; cook, stirring constantly, just until bubbly. Stir in milk and evaporated milk; continue cooking and stirring until thick and bubbling, about 3 minutes. Add horseradish and almonds, stir. Serve warm over grilled fish.

Sauterne Sauce

A wine-sparkled white sauce to pour over grilled trout or salmon which can be made right on the barbecue.

1/4 cup butter *59mL*
1/4 cup chopped green onion
   59mL
1/4 cup all pupose flour *59mL*
1½ cup milk *354mL*

1/2 cup Sauterne wine *118mL*
1 tsp salt *5mL*
1 tsp thyme *5mL*
1/4 tsp white pepper *1.25mL*

Sauté green onion in butter until soft using a small saucepan. Stir in flour and cook, stirring all the time, until mixture bubbles, then add milk, gradually and wine, also in small amounts so that the milk does not curdle; season with salt, thyme and pepper. Continue cooking, stirring all the time, until sauce thickens and bubbles for about 3 minutes. Simmer on back of grill for 10 minutes then serve warm over fish.

Cold sauces which can be made ahead to serve with seafood, are especially good on a hot day. Some food, like lobster and shrimp, is best served with individual dishes of dipping sauce.

London Seafood Sauce

When we visited England a few years ago we had the best prawns with avocados that we had ever tasted. The sauce was the key ingredient and we tried for years to find one similar in the stores at home. Then one day I watched how my friend Helen mixed mustard and mayo (below) and decided to try to duplicate that English sauce. The first step was ketchup and mayonnaise and, glory be, I had it. It works and has wowed some pretty good cooks in its time. Great with lobster and prawns.

mayonnaise (your favourite brand — we use Miracle Whip) ketchup or tomato sauce

Blend ketchup into mayonnaise until it reaches a pinky orange colour. Let sit for at least one hour for flavors to blend.

Note: I suggest you experiment to get the combination of flavors you like. It can be "fancied up" by adding chopped parsley, chives or dill.

Helen's Lobster Topper

mustard
mayonnaise

Flavor mayonnaise with mustard and serve as a dipping sauce for lobster.

Tropical Dip for Prawns

Squeeze lime juice over grilled prawns, then dunk in this dip for exquisite eating. It's nutritional too.

1 small banana
1 medium-size ripe avocado,
  peeled
1 medium-size ripe mango,
  papaya or 2 peaches

zest and juice of 1 large lime
1 tbsp pineapple or orange juice
  15mL
limes to garnish

Just before serving put all ingredients, except garnish limes, in food processor or blender and process until almost smooth. To serve, hollow out an avocado and fill with dip or put in a small bowl. Place in center of serving platter and surround with prawns and wedges of lime. Squeeze lime juice over prawns before dipping.

Red Pepper and Tomato Dipping Sauce

A good sauce for dipping shellfish which have been grilled in their shells or steamed in foil. It's colorful and has a rather pleasant taste with a tang of horseradish.

1 clove garlic minced
1 tbsp olive oil *15mL*
pinch salt (optional)
1 cup tomatoes, finely chopped,
  seeded, peeled *236mL*
1 cup sweet red pepper, finely
  chopped *236mL*

1 tbsp horseradish *15mL*
2 tsp red wine vinegar *10mL*
1 tsp chopped fresh oregano
  5mL
5 coriander seeds, finely crushed
  (use a dry mini-chopper)
pepper, to taste

In a small bowl combine garlic, oil and salt; mix well. Stir in tomatoes, red pepper, horseradish, vinegar, oregano, coriander and pepper. Cover tightly and refrigerate for at least one hour before using. Stores refrigerated for up to 48 hours.

Lemon Sauce

1/3 cup mayonnaise *79mL*
1 tsp prepared horseradish *5mL*
1 tsp prepared mustard *5mL*

2 tbsp lemon juice *10mL*
zest of one lemon (see index)
parsley

Mix all together. Keep cool until served.

Lemon Cream Sauce

1/2 cup sour cream *118mL*
1 package 4 oz cream cheese
   113g pkg
3 tsp lemon juice *15mL*
3 tsp parsley, chopped fine *15mL*

1 tsp grated lemon rind *5mL*
1 tsp horseradish *5mL*
1/4 tsp salt *1.25mL*

Combine all ingredients and chill.

Tartar Sauce

1 cup mayonnaise *236mL*
1 tbsp chopped capers *15mL*
1 tbsp chopped olives *15mL*

1 tbsp chopped pickles *15mL*
1 tbsp parsley *15mL*

Combine all ingredients just prior to serving.

Seafood Cocktail Sauce

1/2 cup chili sauce *118mL*
1/3 cup ketchup *79mL*

1/3 cup prepared horseradish
   79mL
1½ tsp Worcestershire sauce
   7.5mL

Combine all ingredients.

East India Smother

This recipe was given to me years ago by a friend who had come to Canada from India. He used much more curry powder than this. I advise trying it and adjusting to taste.

1 tsp curry powder *5mL*
2 tbsp brandy *30mL*

1/2 cup mayonnaise *118mL*
2-3 tbsp chutney *30-45mL*

Mix all together and place in a pottery crock, chill at least two hours to allow flavors to blend. Place grilled fish fillets on plate and smother them with sauce. Serve with grilled vegetables and fruit.

Cucumber/Dill Sauce

This is good when poured over white fish, or brushed over fish in the last few minutes of cooking.

1/4 cup dairy sour cream *59mL*
1/4 cup mayonnaise *59mL*
3/4 cup peeled, diced cucumber
   (no seeds) *177mL*
1 tbsp cup green onion, chopped
   15mL

1 tsp grated lemon rind *5mL*
1 tbsp fresh dill or 1/4 tsp dried
   dill *15mL*
pepper to taste (optional)

Mix all together, cover and chill to blend flavors before using. Brush on cooking fillets or steaks and serve remainder with fish.

Quicker Cucumber Sauce

1 cup grated cucumber, no peel
   or seeds *236mL*

1 cup mayonnaise *236mL*
2 tbsp chopped fresh dill *30mL*

In a sieve sprinkle cucumber lightly with salt and toss well. Let stand to drain for about 20 minutes. Rinse under cold running water then pat dry on paper towels. Combine three ingredients in serving bowl.

Combine oil, parsley, pepper strips, 2 tbsp/30 mL lemon juice, oregano, 1 tsp/5mL capers and salt in saucepan and cook over low heat for 5 minutes, stirring occasionally. Add more lemon juice or capers, if desired, after tasting. Can be prepared 2 weeks ahead, covered and refrigerated. Serve at room temperature.

Piquant Sauce

1/2 cup olive oil *118mL*
1/2 cup minced fresh parsley
   (Italian preferred) *118mL*
1/2 cup pickled red bell pepper
   strips, drained and diced
   118mL
1/3 cup thinly sliced green onion
   79mL

2 to 3 tbsp lemon juice *30-45mL*
2 tbsp minced fresh oregano
   30mL
or 1 tsp dried, crumbled *5mL*
1 to 2 tbsp capers, drained and
   rinsed *15-30mL*
salt

Combine oil, parsley, pepper strips, onion, 2 tbsp/20mL lemon juice, oregano, 1 tsp/4mL capers and salt in saucepan and cook over low heat for 5 minutes, stirring occasionally. Add more lemon juice or capers, if desired, after tasting. Can be prepared 2 weeks ahead, covered and refrigerated. Serve at room temperature.

SALSAS

Salsas are becoming a favored accompaniment for grilled foods, and fish is no exception. Easily made, they are also low in fat and calories, which may account for some of the popularity.

Salsas are sauces that are fresh vegetable or fruit based. They generally have a chopped consistency which evidences the original fruit or vegetable used to make them. In fact they come together very easily and quickly by using a food processor and they can be stored for several days.

Salsas are normally served cold or at room temperature and to my mind resemble the chutneys I remember from Britain, the main difference being the fact that they are not cooked or preserved and reflect ingredients from another locale. Being Mexican in origin, salsas call for lots of exotic ingredients most easily found in the west and south. However items such as Jalapeno peppers are becoming more widely available all the time. My suggestion is that you talk to the people where you buy your vegetables and ask them to identify the various peppers and specialty ingredients.

Easy Tomato Salsa

1 can (16 oz) Italian style plum tomatoes or 3 large fresh tomatoes, peeled and seeded *1 can 480mL*

1 can (4 oz) mild or hot green chilies, drained *1 can 120mL*

1 small onion, quartered

1 small clove garlic

3 tbsp fresh parsley leaves *45mL*

3 tbsp fresh coriander (cilantro) leaves *45mL* or 1 1/2 tbsp dried leaves *22.5mL*

Hot Pepper sauce to taste

Put tomatoes, chilies, onion and garlic into food processor or blender. Process until coarsley chopped. Add parsley and coriander. Process just to mix. Add hot pepper sauce to taste. Refrigerate covered up to 3 days.

Citrus Salsa

I like adding parsley to this salsa because of the green flecks it gives when served over a white fish steak. If the purity of the orange/ yellow appeals, leave it out. A mini-chopper greatly aids in preparation. Can be made up to 24 hours ahead. Great with grilled fish.

1 cup finely minced white onion
   236mL
1/3 cup seasoned rice wine
   vinegar *79mL*
1/2 cup fresh orange juice
   118mL
2 tbsp minced orange zest *30mL*

juice of one lemon
zest of 2 lemons, minced
1 tbsp minced fresh ginger *15mL*
2 oranges, completely peeled
   and coarsley chopped
1/2 cup fresh parsley, chopped
   (optional) *118mL*

Combine all ingredients in a bowl, in the order given.

Note: ZEST of lemon, lime or orange is the outer skin of the fruit. The best way to "zest" a fruit is with a zester, a gadget with a handle like a paring knife which you draw over the skin. You can grate or use a very sharp knife, but you must be sure to leave behind all the white inner skin. Zesting with the correct utensil gives long strips of rind, mince these when using in a marinade.

    When a recipe calls for GRATED CITRUS PEEL, use your zester and then chop strips fine for best results.

Green Chutney with Avocados and Peppers

This recipes comes to me from fellow cookbook writer, Kasey Wilson of the west coast, who is always up on the food trends. It is smooth enough to be served as an accent on grilled trout, on grilled fish steaks or with an omelet.

6 jalapeno peppers, roasted and
   peeled
4 red bell peppers, roasted and
   peeled
3 avocados, peeled
2 cups lightly packed coriander
   leaves (cilantro) *472mL*

3/4 cup lightly packed parsley
   177mL
lime juice to taste
3 cloves garlic
3/4 tsp garam masala; recipe
   follows
dash sugar
dash salt

Cut both peppers and the avocados into a 1/4-inch/.64cm cubes. In a food processor combine the rest of the ingredients into a smooth paste. Gently stir in the peppers and avocados and serve.

Garam Masala:

1/4 cup ground cumin *59mL*
2 tbsp whole cloves *30mL*
2 tbsp grated nutmeg *30mL*
2 tbsp curry powder *30mL*

Combine all ingredients in a blender or mini-chopper and blend well. It will keep tightly covered for up to two months and can be used in place of plain curry powder for an Indian accent in many dishes.

BASTING SAUCES

Oyster Sauce

Excellent for basting most fish, especially shark, catfish and halibut.

1 tbsp oyster sauce *15mL*
1 tbsp ketchup *15mL*
1 tsp Worcestershire sauce *5mL*

Mix all ingredients together. Brush both sides of fish while barbecuing.

Dill Sauce

A tangy sauce, ideal for strong-flavored fish such as shark, swordfish and mackerel.

1 tbsp lemon juice *15mL*
1 tbsp horseradish *15mL*
1 tbsp minced onion *15mL*
1/2 tsp dill weed *2.5mL*

Mix all ingredients together. Baste seafood with mixture while grilling.

Barbecue Sauce

An easy way to spice up seafood.

1/2 cup soft butter *118mL*
2 tbsp lemon juice *30mL*
1/2 tsp sweet basil *2.5mL*

1 tsp dill seed *5mL*
1/2 tsp salt *2.5mL*
1/4 tsp cayenne *1.25mL*

Mix all ingredients together in a small bowl. Refrigerate for 2-3 hours to allow flavors to develop. Brush on fish before and after grilling.

Aussie Rum Orange Kebab Baste

An Australian visitor gave me this recipe which her family uses on kebabs which have fruit on them. We tried it on kebabs with shark and a mixture of fruits and it was delicious. Teams well with Pina Coladas or Strawberry Margueritas, prawn and fruit kebabs and shark steaks for a summer theme meal.

zest and juice of 1 orange (about
    1/2 cup/*118mL of juice*)
2 tsp lemon juice *10mL*
and 2 strokes of lemon zest

1/4 cup honey *59mL*
2 tbsp dark rum *30mL*
pinch cinnamon

Combine all ingriedients in a glass jar and allow to sit for at least one hour before using to baste kebabs or fruit in a grill basket.

SPECIALTY BUTTERS

Unless otherwise stated, have butter at room temperature to begin.

Butters can be spread on fish or vegetables to be wrapped in foil and grilled. Brush on cooked side of fish after it has been turned to prevent it from drying or brush on just as you serve fish. Or, mold or roll and serve on the side.

Lemon Garlic Butter

1/4 lb butter *113 g*
1 large garlic clove, minced fine

1/2 lemon

Remove the zest from the lemon. Squeeze juice over butter then cream in the garlic and zest.

Quick Garlic Butter

1/4 cup butter *59 mL*
1/2 tsp garlic powder *2.5 mL*

2 heads fresh parsley, minced
or
1 tsp dried parsley *5 mL*

Mix together.

Tarragon Garlic Butter

1/3 cup butter *79 mL*
2 cloves garlic, minced
2 green onion, chopped fine
   (tops too)

1/4 tsp dried tarragon *1.25 mL*
salt
black pepper

Mix all ingredients together and refrigerate until ready to use.

Tarragon Butter

Make the above substituting 1 tbsp/15 mL parsley for the garlic.

Lemony Sesame Butter

Melt 1/2 cup/118 mL butter; squeeze in the juice of one-half lemon, zest the rind and add; then add 1 tbsp/15 mL sesame seeds. Stir before using to baste fish steaks on the grill. Drizzle a little over fish on plate just before serving.

Orange Butter

Mix together finely grated orange rind and softened butter. Generally one orange to 1/4 cup/59 mL butter.

Mexibutter

This is delicious spread on shellfish, poached fish or hot corn on the cob.

1 small sweet red pepper	1 clove garlic, minced
1 hot cherry or jalapeno pepper	2 tbsp sour cream *30 mL*
1 cup butter (room temperature) *236 mL*	squeezed lime juice

Broil red and hot cherry peppers 4 inches/10 cm from heat, turning often, for about 10 minutes for hot cherry pepper and 20 minutes for red pepper or until blackened and blistered all over. Place in paper bag and close tightly or cover with tea towel; let steam for 10 minutes. Let cool; peel, seed and finely chop.

In a small bowl whip butter lightly with a fork. Blend in peppers, garlic, sour cream and lime juice. Either put into a crock or place on waxed paper and shape into a log and chill.

Blue-Cheese Butter

I especially like this over tender shark steaks.

1/2 cup blue or Roquefort cheese *118 mL*	2 tbsp sherry, white wine, brandy or cream *30 mL*
1/4 cup butter *59 mL*	

Crumble the cheese and let it and butter stand at room temperature for about 1 hour. Mash together using a fork gradually adding liquid ingredient. Stir until a smooth paste forms then put into a serving bowl.

Variation: Add 1/4 cup ground almonds or 1 green onion, finely chopped.

Caraway Butter

1/2 cup butter, softened *118 mL*   1/2 tsp caraway seeds, crushed
2 tbsp minced parsley *30 mL*   *2.5 mL*
                                                              2 tbsp lemon juice *30 mL*

Blend first 3 ingredients in a small bowl, then gradually drizzle in lemon juice, beating well until all are combined. Turn onto wax paper and roll into a log, or put into a mold and chill until firm. Slice to serve on grilled fish.

Mustard Shallot Butter

Excellent used with grilled swordfish, shark or halibut steaks.

4 tbsp unsalted butter, at room   1 large shallot, minced
   temperature *60 mL*   1/4 tsp salt *1.25 mL*
1 tbsp grainy mustard such as   1/4 tsp white pepper *1.25 mL*
   Pommery or Dijon with seeds
   15 mL

Cream together all ingredients until well blended. Just before removing grilled fish from grill, daub on a pat of butter. Serve as it starts to melt.

Anchovy Butter

Cream together a little anchovy paste, butter and lemon juice to taste. Served with grilled fish.

Special Breads

Garlic Bread

loaf of French or Italian Bread,
unsliced

garlic butter
foil

Use a bread knife to slash the bread as if slicing without going right through bottom crust. Spread garlic butter on both sides of each slice. Wrap tightly in heavy-duty aluminum foil and place on grill over medium-hot coals. You can place on the warming shelf if you plan on closing barbecue lid, but it may take longer to cook. Turn often if on grill, so that the bottom doesn't burn.

African Hot Loaf

1 small French loaf
1/4 cup soft butter *59 mL*

1 small onion, minced
1/2 tsp Tabasco pepper sauce
1.25 mL

Mix butter, onion and Tabasco sauce. Cut the loaf into thin slices and spread with the butter mix. Wrap loaf in foil and heat through (as above). Serve hot.

Leslie's Tuna Loaf

I named this for my cousin who introduced me to the delights of grilled tuna and cheese sandwiches more years ago than either of us want to think about. It's great if you have kids who are not fussy on grown up food, but are tired of weiners. Some corn on the cob and a tuna loaf and they will be happy and "well" fed.

loaf of French or Italian Bread   celery, chopped fine
tuna   mayonnaise
onion, chopped fine (optional)   tomato (optional)
cheese slices   butter

Slice loaf into 1/2 inch/1 cm slices, without cutting through bottom crust. Mix tuna with minced onion, mayonnaise and celery. Think about this before you do it. You are going to cut this apart into sandwiches after its cooked so you have to leave every other slice with no filling.

Butter or spread mayonnaise on two sides of a "pocket", then spread tuna mixture on one side, place a slice of cheese and tomatoes and lightly press together. Miss the next slice, and repeat until loaf is filled. Wrap securely with aluminum foil and grill for about 20 minutes over medium-hot coals.

INDEX